Praise for:

The Visionary Brand: *The Success Formula Behind the World's Most Visionary Brands*

"Exceptionally well written, organized, and presented, The Visionary Brand must be considered essential reading for all aspiring entrepreneurs and corporate executives seeking to expand their market share.

The Visionary Brand is unreservedly recommended for community, corporate, college, university library Business Management instructional reference collections, and for the personal reading lists of entrepreneurs, MBA students, and corporate executives."

James Cox, Editor-in-Chief,
Midwest Book Review

"Exploring the concept of a 'Visionary' brand, the book explores the building blocks that successful brands have used to create a vision for their products, a consistent presentation of that vision across the years, and a culture of loyal and engaged followers.

The book aims to provide a practical framework for studying successful real-world cases with a focus on authenticity, creativity, and building a brand based on ethics and principles. I'm confident that readers of his work will be able to take the insight they gain from this book and apply it to their brands.

Encompassing macro and micro styles of thinking about brand management, *The Visionary Brand: The Success Formula Behind the World's Most Visionary Brands* is an essential tool for setting the short and long-term goals that will lead your organization to ongoing success in the future.
Overall, I would strongly recommend this book to those in a position of leadership in business who wish to understand how to take their organization to a new level."

K.C. Finn, Award Winning,
Bestselling Author

"A great mix of inspiration and practical advice on brand building and business in general, I would definitely recommend!"

Sarah Hurley,
Award-Winning Entrepreneur

"The Visionary Brand: The Success Formula Behind the World's Most Visionary Brands belongs in any business collection focused on branding success and makes a case for fostering a visionary, market-driving force that achieves through innovation and inspiration.

From product visions and engagement choices to creating a disruptive, different brand that stands out from the crowd, Bryan Smeltzer provides a series of cautions that cover the processes of a successful formula for transformation and change.

What makes for "a truly visionary brand as opposed to one that loses its way" lies at the heart of these discussions, which encourage visionary thinkers not just to identify visionary qualities and pursuits but understand what leads to success and what threatens failure.

Smeltzer's three decades in business lend a practical, real-world side to his theories and visions. These help fellow business visionaries understand the foundations of identifying what elements are involved in a successful visionary brand.

Business collections will find his book specific and filled with opportunities that visionary thinkers will find enlightening and inspirational, grounded in the nuts and bolts of real-world experience."

D. Donovan, Senior Reviewer,
Midwest Book Review

"This book is both: inspiring and practical. It covers visionary brand concepts and how to achieve success in building one."

Darya Yegorina, C-Level Executive,
Blogger/Influencer

"The Visionary Brand outlines what it takes to build a true, authentic visionary brand. It provides actionable insight and entertaining case studies that can support you in taking your brand to the next level and beyond!"

Chris Lupo, Director-Sports Marketing,
Rudy Project

"*The Visionary Brand* is a welcome, real-world overview of how a brand manager is an '...orchestra leader...' and I can't wait to share this title with my students in my branding classes."

> **Robert Hughes**, Professor/Educator,
> University of Florida

"*The Visionary Brand* provides fantastic insight on what separates commonplace brands from the visionary ones, all taken from an 'inside perspective,' truly inspiring."

> **Jeff Yearous**, CEO/President,
> DZYNIT

"Loved it! *The Visionary Brand: The Success Formula Behind the World's Most Visionary Brands* outlines the independent elements to emulate and successfully execute the foundational strategies used by iconic brands.

Many believe that a formula has set certain iconic brands above the rest. Brands like Nike, Adidas, and Apple have used a combination of culture, innovation, product, and marketing to give them a competitive edge. In *The Visionary Brand: The Success Formula Behind the World's Most Visionary Brands*, Bryan Smeltzer outlines the independent elements an individual can successfully execute to achieve this foundational strategy.

With nearly three decades of experience in business, Bryan Smeltzer is qualified to provide the information in this book. The author founded and successfully sold his own company, and has been in executive roles with iconic brands, so he is someone I have no problems listening to for strategic advice."

> **Madene Carr**, Author, Business Leader
> Adjunct Faculty

The Visionary Brand

The Success Formula Behind the World's Most
Visionary Brands

Bryan Smeltzer

LIQUIDMIND PRESS

Smeltzer, Bryan
The visionary brand: the success formula behind the
world's most visionary brands / Bryan Smeltzer.

ISBN: 978-1-7371881-0-0

Published in the United States of America

First published in 2022 by LiquidMind Press

To those who aspire to greatness and have a vision for what the future should be, this book is for you.

Embrace your vision
Commit to being different
Inspire others
Aspire to be a Visionary!

Table of Contents:

Introduction 1
Becoming Visionary 3

The Journey 9

The Brand 15
Evolution 17
Loyalty 20
Pillars 22

The Vision Paradox 26
Breakaway Product Pipeline 28
Foresight 30
Revolution . . . Recreate . . . 32

The Elements Of A Successful Formula 34
The Creative Engine 37
Market-Driving Vs. Market-Driven 40
Be Disruptive 42
Be Different 46
Case Study: Category Disruption 49
The Positioning 52
Selling Your Soul 54
Bloodlines 58
The Best 60
Loyalty Loop 63
Strategic Competitiveness 68
Promote A Lifestyle 73

The Omni-Channel Strategy 77

The Power Triad 86

The Culture Matrix 97
Culture And Leadership 102

The Product Vision 110
Innovate, Don't Imitate 112
Create Breakaway Products 117
Build A Drawdown Product Pipeline 123
Lead Through Extinction 130
The Brand Is The Product 134
Take Risks 138

The Ecosystem 145

The Fuel 150
Inspire Through Personalization 155
Brand Ambassadors 157

The UX 162
Engagement 167
Empathize 169

The New Age 173
Disruptive Revolution 176
Visionary Legacy 178

The Artist 180

The Courage 187
Destiny 193
Live Your Dream 195

Summary 197

Index 202

INTRODUCTION

Oakley had a problem.

Over the previous decades, it had established itself as a titan in the world of eyewear thanks to its tenacious, take-no-prisoners culture. It was everything a brand aspires to be: it pushed the boundaries of the industry, setting the pace and letting its competitors try to play catch-up, all supported by a dedicated community of brand ambassadors who were only too happy to be part of the aspirational, active Oakley lifestyle.

But there was just one problem: their community went wild for their culture and design, but there were several related product categories that were going untapped. While Oakley eyewear was a study in breakthrough products that drove the market, the apparel, footwear and accessories (AFA) product line extensions were not part of the brand's portfolio. The company was sure they could take on other action sports brands and build a successful business where one did not exist today. Quiksilver and Billabong, among other action sports brands, were taking the lion's share of those markets. Oakley said, "We can do that, too!"

A plan was put in place, and the categories were launched. The product teams were given the go-ahead to launch a whole new line of Oakley-branded AFA products. The eyewear division would keep doing what they were doing so well, and the AFA teams would get the resources needed to build the brand bigger than ever. In short order, Oakley was ready to begin a new chapter in their dominance of these new market opportunities.

And that's when Oakley's little problem became a much bigger problem—one that would alienate some of their core community and drive the entire brand culture in a different direction. Both category authenticity and channel distribution would quickly become problems whereas they hadn't been before. Oakley began to lose its cultural direction, as well as those loyal brand ambassadors who stuck with the brand through its evolution over the decades. They had loved and embraced the brand for what it was, not what it was becoming.

In the end, Oakley was more fortunate than most brands that go down a similar road—trying to be something they are not. After making the decision to dedicate themselves to creating what was right for the brand and aligning with their brand identity, they were able to regain their customers' trust and brand equity, and were finally able to climb their way back to the top of their core product categories.

Most brands don't get a second chance like that—Oakley was only able to manage it because the visionaries steering the brand had the courage to reflect on what had happened so they could learn from what did not work and get back to what did work—doing what is right for the brand and their loyal customers.

Even global, iconic brands can end up losing sight of their cultural bloodlines if they are not committed to the foundational pillars on which their brands were built. No matter how solid the product, marketing, and sales—no matter how powerful your formula for success—without a singular guiding vision at the helm determining what is right for the brand, what will drive it forward into the next generation?

In other words, Oakley learned early on what it takes to be a truly visionary brand as opposed to one that loses its way.

BECOMING VISIONARY

Over my nearly three decades in business—from founding my own company to successfully selling it to being involved in executive-level roles with some of the world's most iconic brands—I have come across brands that have visionary qualities. But ultimately, none have had all that is required to achieve authentic visionary brand status. Somewhere in the brand, something is almost always missing. Even brands like Under Armour and Oakley—ones that build themselves up to the top of their industry—can lose sight of their future when they abandon the principles that made them great in the first place. Ultimately, no matter how strong a brand may be in a dozen different capacities, all things considered, it is an incredibly difficult task to achieve and sustain a visionary brand.

When asked about what makes a brand *visionary*, most people will come up with three or four common traits associated with a brand:

Product

Marketing

Culture

Innovation

These are good starting points, but each on its own does not make for a visionary brand, nor do all four put together. To achieve visionary status, you must not only have these core qualities, but all must be built in as an integral part of your brand's foundation. That foundation needs to be structurally upheld by foundational pillars that support your vision in every aspect of the brand's actions—both internally and with the world at large.

Throughout my years, I have always been curious as to what makes a genuinely visionary brand. There are qualities like the four mentioned above, but in reality, it takes the vertical integration of many different pieces to make a brand run on all cylinders effectively. You may have a Lamborghini that looks fast, but if you are only running on six cylinders, you are missing out on its full potential. And so it goes with brands; some are six cylinders, some eight . . . but I have yet to see one that runs on all twelve over the long haul.

That's not to say becoming a visionary brand is impossible—however, it is a continual struggle to establish and live up to the pillars your brand was founded on. Above all else, being visionary involves touching, impacting, and energizing all aspects of your company—all the bloodlines that flow through the veins of a living, breathing organ called a brand.

As the leader of a brand, you're essentially acting as an orchestra conductor: you're not just leading individuals with different talents in their independent tasks, but synthesizing their talents and efforts toward the singular goal of collectively making music as a unit. Depending on your actions and your vision, the result can be either harmonious or disastrous.

At the end of the day, it is your responsibility to ensure each player in the orchestra is correctly prepared, synchronized, and in harmony with one another. How you lead the ensemble can be translated to a brand's eventual success. Where there is a common goal, along with preparation and coordination, beautiful things happen at all levels. Although challenging, having a shared vision—led from the top down and anchored in guiding and values-driven principles—ensures everyone involved will be committed to achieving success.

Or to employ another metaphor: I often refer to those visionaries who have been able to achieve this brand status as "five-star generals." They are few in number, and each has successfully led their teams into battles and achieved many victories. Obviously, leading a brand is not the same as going to war, but this gives you some idea of the kind of difficulties you will encounter as you move through the different stages of brand development. You will face choices that test your foundational, visionary principles, ones that will affect the future of your brand. As a result of your choices, your brand will continue to grow and develop . . . or it will deteriorate before the eyes of your team and your supporters.

Understanding the growth of a brand is a trait not easily discovered, which is why so few true visionaries exist. I have found that brands that have sustained growth—not just revenue, but also brand equity—tend to have this trait in common. Brands that have nurtured the soul of their company are the ones that provide value in the eyes of the consumer. This value may be realized through the products a brand sells, and likewise through the brand's culture or the aspirational lifestyle they market to their community. Each delivers a different loyalty curve or experience to that brand advocate.

The key to building a lasting brand truly is loyalty. We live in a world where loyalty is considered one of the inherent values of every company; betray that trust to your stakeholders or your customers and you lose their loyalty. Betray your foundational visionary principles of the brand and you lose loyalty. Remember, selling a brand means selling a lifestyle you can touch and feel, and when trust is damaged, it is challenging to repair.

But where does this loyalty come from? Ultimately, loyalty is traced back to the **visionary**—the one who sets the foundational pillars and principles of the brand and what the brand stands for across all areas of its existence—be it product, messaging, or culture. Each of these three areas carries the torch of the brand vision, and they are all integral parts of defining its future.

My main purpose in writing this book is to break down how to achieve and maintain visionary status as a brand and what this looks like in real life. It's important to know that a truly, fully visionary brand is an incredibly rare thing. Steve Jobs, Jeff Bezos, Bill Gates, Andrew Carnegie, John D. Rockefeller—each of these individuals was a truly visionary leader, and their brands broke barriers and revolutionized their respective industries. Yet each of their brands also missed at least one piece of the puzzle. Some grew complacent in their success and allowed their brand to be overtaken by competitors; others may have had revolutionary products, but lacked the human touch to carry their discoveries into the lives of their customers. This is a real lesson for anyone with the desire to build a visionary brand: it is an ongoing journey, one that doesn't stop no matter what level of market success is achieved.

Through my research and real-life experiences with iconic brands, I found I have been able to piece together the formula of what constitutes a true, all-cylinders-firing visionary brand. I've included plenty of examples of brands that are running on most cylinders, and a few that drive with much less—both of which are great examples of what to do and what not to do. Most of all, in this book I lay out foundational principles shared by brands that have successfully navigated the barriers to long-term success put in front of them.

Through my decades of direct experience with these brands, along with the hard knocks and success I encountered along the way, I hope you will find *The Visionary Brand* either inspires you in building your brand or reinvigorates a passion inside of you to realign your goals for you and your team. This is not a goal for the faint of heart; the journey will take courage, trust, and commitment to your foundation pillars to ensure your success. Yet ultimately, everyone has the ability to achieve visionary status. Those who succeed persevere; those who fail compromise.

Fear is the opposite of courage, and those who succeed choose courage—the courage to stand when others fall. If you have the courage to stick to your guns and create, build, and grow your brand while sticking to your pillars of success . . . then read on, visionary!

THE JOURNEY

Everyone's journey toward building a visionary brand is different. However, most successful journeys will have a few things in common. By following the journey of a successful or visionary brand leader with an open mind and a desire to learn, you'll have the chance to internalize some key lessons to inspire you on your own journey.

Personally, I've been fortunate enough to learn from some of the greatest brands in the world. Throughout this learning process, I was notorious for asking a million questions:

"How does this provide ongoing value to our customers?"

"What is our go-to-market strategy?"

"Does this degrade brand equity?"

Although this habit was time-consuming, asking questions is what allowed me to gain a solid foundation very early on in my career.

Having graduated with an engineering degree, I quickly found my true passion was not in the aerospace industry, but instead in consumer products. I immediately found myself passionate about the lifestyle these brands provided, even more so than the products themselves. Growing up with a family entrenched in the sports lifestyle, being a multi-sport athlete and a former college football player, and having a very active lifestyle, this was a natural transition for me. However, little did I know how difficult this transition would be, or how treacherous the entrepreneurial path it would take me down.

This journey would start with designing a new dual-density sport sandal, but quickly moved to finding a niche in a distribution channel I found aligned well with my background: NCAA licensing. The concept was to provide a better men's and ladies' collection licensed with the most prestigious, passionate universities in the country. This would prove not only to be one of the greatest learning experiences of my life but would also allow me to enter an industry I have always had a passion for: the consumer products apparel and footwear industry. Getting into this industry let me work with and for such iconic consumer brands as adidas, Oakley, and TaylorMade, to reference a few.

This journey was the optimum learning experience. From an industry where technical design and engineering prowess were critical to success, I moved to an industry where the ability to market a lifestyle and product points of difference was integral to ongoing category leadership. I learned the apparel and footwear business from observing, doing, and educating myself on what would allow me the best chance for success. It was also critical to understand the how of designing, creating, and commercializing products.

After this firsthand education, over ten years I was able to build a company from the ground up, starting with nothing. It is rewarding to create something of value to others; to me, a true entrepreneurial journey—going from something from nothing to something—and even the word "entrepreneur" is sacred. It is not so much a matter of building, but rather creating from scratch. This creation process is inherently risky, and those who have crossed this chasm have experienced what it takes to achieve success through overcoming barriers—barriers not experienced by those who have not been part of a startup. Being an entrepreneur is a badge of honor, one not quickly or easily earned. I always say that entrepreneurs are inherently not risk-takers, but rather are risk *assessors* and *eliminators*.

I was able to learn many lessons along the way to successfully run an apparel business. First and foremost, how to reduce mistakes—not to eliminate them entirely, as this is neither feasible nor desirable. Those who do not fail are the ones who take no risks. This road to success is a path built from failure, and one held upon the shoulders of those who execute the plan seamlessly.

It is from these experiences with globally recognized brands that I was able to gain in-depth industry knowledge on what makes a great brand succeed. Each brand had its own unique culture, products, and positioning, and each experience was a building block in defining what makes a visionary brand.

With each of these brands, I was leading product teams in marketing, business development, and sales. This broad spectrum of experience within these brands allowed me to observe the inner workings behind these machines. This is a perspective others may not have exposure to, but ultimately one I hope to translate in this book. Having been in a dynamic, diverse, disruptive culture—and seeing a brand as a living, breathing thing that must be protected—gave me a new perspective on what it entails to be a visionary.

When it comes down to it, the long-term livelihood of the brand sits in the lap of the visionary. The visionary is the heart that drives the blood through the veins of the entire brand. This living thing we call a brand needs nurturing for it to grow. We'll look at just what this looks like throughout the book.

Generational products do not come along frequently, but inevitably when they do it has been the result of a visionary mindset—someone who carried this idea in their head and was able to turn their vision into reality. This can only happen through a specific order of small steps that eventually bring an idea to its summit. The journey is not easy, and will leave cuts and bruises along the way, but none so devastating that they make the journey impossible to complete.

It's a funny thing, but your journey to a visionary brand must be defined in detail without really knowing the end result. It sounds like an oxymoron, but it is the reality of having visionary foresight that when a path is closed, you build another one until you get to your eventual destination. Just do not change your forward-thinking direction, as that is the path to reality.

Steve Jobs was notorious for his so-called "reality distortion field," but he was indeed able to bring this distortion to reality. If this was never achieved by Jobs pushing to achieve his vision, Apple might have been another brand whose destiny was in the graveyard of lost dreams.

My own journey took many paths, and each road or detour led me to this destination. There were times along my journey where I wanted to turn around, but what I found is these barriers are roadblocks to those who do not have the perseverance to achieve what is seemingly impossible until it is accomplished.

This firsthand knowledge, along with what I learned from smarter people than myself, has allowed me to create what I feel is a definitive guide to achieving visionary brand status. Having the traits I picked up along my journey is key to continuing to sustain and maintain a long-term vision, deliver value to your consumers, and sustain your brand.

Enjoy the journey!

Your destiny awaits!

THE BRAND

What makes a brand a brand? Is it . . .

Product?

Marketing?

Culture?

Innovation?

Each of these can certainly be a foundational piece of the make-up of a brand, and consumer perceptions are built on these separate components. However, I found in most instances, consumers perceive a brand as a **lifestyle,** comprised of many different aspects both inspirational and aspirational, or as a **commodity**, which serves a specific need or purpose. For example, when Nike created the "Just Do It" or "Bo Knows" campaigns, Nike created both an inclusionary active lifestyle and persona that allowed them to sell products, creating a culture built around demonstrating an inspirational lifestyle. These campaigns reflect its culture, which is made up of a community of like-minded athletes working towards the same aspirational goal. In other words, it sells a lifestyle more than it sells individual goods. And selling a lifestyle is now more important than ever for a successful brand.

In this new age of retail, brands are able to control their own destiny more easily than the traditional brick-and-mortar retailers. Until recently the destination was the door; now it is accomplished through e-comm, providing a direct relationship with the customer not available previously. The most interesting upshot of this change is brands are now embracing what used to be the fortress of retailers: opening their own stores and competing directly with them. This is very threatening to retailers, as it allows brands to cannibalize product assortments, but more importantly, to control their own destiny through direct distribution and direct relationship-building with their customers. Brands now have the opportunity to control both their products' User Experience (UX) and brand loyalty in their entirety. Prior to this strategy, retailers would control much of the customers' purchase experience, with most times the activation not matching the experience brands would like to have created.

Exploiting this new relationship with consumers has proven very successful for brands, and retailers have no choice but to compete with premium brands through e-comm to balance the scales of commerce as much in their favor as possible. Not an easy task; brands have pricing power, community following, and product pipelines to draw from, while retail does not. Most importantly, though, there's one key thing to remember:

Unless you ARE a brand, you cannot BE a brand.

The competitive advantage the retail landscape had was the ability to provide one-stop shopping. In light of new challenges posed by the changing marketplace, some retailers have not stood still. In addition to embracing e-comm, they have decided to create "sub" brands—partnering with companies in a collective effort to produce these traditionally commodity price point products. Some have been successful, but most are miserable failures. The reason for this failure should be obvious given the quote above (and the rest of the book as a whole): no matter the quality of the product you sell, you can't just tack on a brand and expect it to perform like a true premium brand. Premium, fully visionary brands need to be built from the ground up.

The focus of our brand proposition will be on **lifestyle brands** and what makes them visionary. Let's start by looking at the trajectory of how brands have evolved over time.

EVOLUTION

Every brand needs to ensure they are anchored in their core principles—what makes them a brand in the eyes of their consumers—and maintain this vision throughout the cycles of the company's evolution.

A brand is built on a foundation driven predominantly through marketplace positioning and product points of difference . . . but its long-term growth is dependent on its ability to remain flexible, making the job of marketing inherently difficult. After all, consumers' perceptions, attention span, and value determination change literally on a daily basis with dynamic access to information through search engines, targeted marketing campaigns, e-mail offers, blogs, and podcasts (as well as a myriad of other digital channels that are still being developed, such as augmented or virtual reality). Each of these digital channels provides faster access to data, which can benefit how a brand evolves relative to its interactions with the world at large; at the same time, these advances in technology convolute a brand's ability to cut through the noise. A brand needs to cut a clear path to omni-channel messaging that has a clear, defined and tangible return on investment (ROI) in terms of brand equity growth (see the chapter on Omni-Channel Strategy for more on this subject).

If you've somehow missed it, we are in the midst of one of the most historical transformations in the age of retail in our lifetime. This evolution has come at such a rapid pace that most brands were caught off-guard, though, in reality, they should have seen this transformation coming. This is both invigorating for those who are proactive and fatal to those who are paralyzed by how to act when faced with this new reality.

Like evolution in the natural world, only the brands that adapt to these changes are fit enough to survive over the long haul. Those who adapted to this evolution are gaining market share; those who did not are likely in dire need of rescue and on a road to nowhere.

Previously, how brands traditionally engaged with their consumers was through retail distribution. However, this is no longer the case, as direct engagement with consumers has taken a front-row seat. Those who were the early adopters and recognized this evolution are the ones now reaping the rewards; they have already had the time to go through the growth pains associated with any new industry evolution, and now are perfectly positioned for success. The upshot of this change is that brands now control their own destiny, having many ways to directly engage with, acquire, and build loyalty with their **brand advocates** (more on this later).

This direct engagement is a key lifeline for a brand. In order to grow brand loyalty, you must engage, interact with, and reward those who are part of your brand community. This community is now part of your brand family, and having direct access to your customers comes with the need for your community to be both respected and nurtured.

The retail evolution is real, and instead of fear for the future, brands need to embrace the reality. Brands that have positioned themselves to provide a lifestyle experience will have even more opportunities to provide value beyond product. Being able to better control the future is now in the hands of the brand: you can give your brand life by being authentic, or to wither and die for fear of the future or unwillingness to recognize what is in front of you.

LOYALTY

The brand **Loyalty Loop** is something we will discuss in detail in the "Positioning" section. For now, it's important to know that the loyalty loop has turned into a powerful weapon in building a brand's recurring purchase cycle with customers.

Ongoing, authentic engagement by brands is a key ingredient in the perfect mix between advocating and acquiring, both of which are important to the livelihood of a brand. Content that is relevant to your community defines a point of difference from your competition, and is reinforced over a long period of time to sustain success.

Because this relationship can now be measured through various metrics, loyalty is much more meaningful for brands. There are numerous such metrics, but the most important is **retention rate**. Being able to acquire and engage customers is important, but retention is the key to a brand's longevity. Unless a brand builds and maintains a high retention rate, its prospects for long-term success remain shaky.

A brand's loyalty is also determined by its **trust factor**. With the proliferation of digital communications, the literal onslaught of dynamic engagement, along with the massive flow of content, contributes to the need for a brand to provide authentic content. Worse, producing content that is perceived as inauthentic can have the opposite effect, causing significant damage to the trust a brand has built with its customers. Staying true to the brand's vision—and having a clear, concise plan on engagement, positioning and messaging—will bring a cohesiveness that reinforces your trust factor.

Growing a brand is not easy; there are many barriers to entry, and you will run into even more barriers once you feel the barbarians at the gate. This will be the time when you may feel the need to undermine your vision for short-term benefits. Resist this impulse, as doing so will actually cause long-term pain in the form of damaged trust and lost loyalty. It is very difficult if not impossible to gain back trust from your advocate family as a result of such a decision. This wisdom will come up again and again along your journey to visionary status, and I will keep bringing it up in this book—I promise, no matter how many times I mention the importance of staying true to your principles, inevitably some brands (and readers) will be tempted to veer off the path, and without a doubt, they will end up crashing and burning.

Trust is very real, and when abused it has brought down many companies. Being able to manage (not manipulate) this trust is a key principle for sustained success. I say *sustained* success, as many companies have built trust only to lose it, whether due to inadvisable choices, bad luck, or poor timing. Whenever trust is lost, building it up again requires diligence and even more commitment to a company's foundational vision. Once a leak has started, it is best to start patching up the leak before it becomes a flood. Own up to your mistake, earn back trust, and be patient while this process is happening.

All too often, when severe damage occurs to a brand it is self-inflicted. This can come about as a result of not adhering to brand values or forgetting why your advocates joined your brand family. Customers have many choices in this world, and loyalty is as valuable as it is hard to earn; providing a true, authentic, and ongoing experience with your brand is a key focus for creating loyal customers—and should always be a top priority.

Ensure you are always building trust, providing value beyond product, and engaging with those most loyal to the brand. This loyalty will carry you through the hills and valleys you will inevitably encounter as a brand. When the road gets difficult, you will be relieved to know you have nurtured this base.

PILLARS

Every brand that has achieved sustainable long-term success has **foundational pillars** that enable them to thrive. These pillars are unique in their execution, but common to each brand. The seven foundational pillars that make up a brand are:

- **Brand** – how the brand itself is defined
- **Product** – what the brand produces

- **Culture** – how the brand interacts with others and behaves within itself
- **Positioning** – where and at what level the brand sells its product
- **Creators** – who build the brand's future
- **Vision** – the foundational, day-to-day mission that drives the brand's interactions
- **Execution** – the common goal shared by everyone participating in the brand

Each of these pillars is a building block that makes up a brand's foundation, providing a clear path and direction to its future. Every brand has its own unique pillars that are critical to building a rock-solid foundation that provides value to everyone inside and outside the company. These pillars are vertical in that each is necessary for the brand's foundation to be maintained. These principles keep the brand honest with itself and ensure everyone understands the common perceptions, expectations, and ongoing positioning throughout the entire company. Brands thrive when these pillars are upheld, and fail when they are allowed to fall.

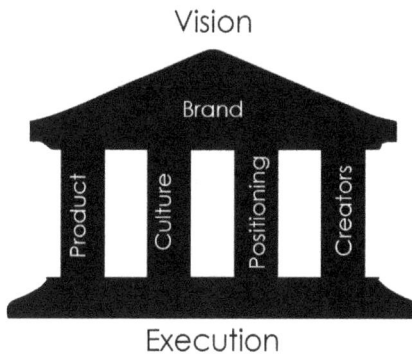

Vision

Brand

Product Culture Positioning Creators

Execution

Foundational Pillars

Brands that reach the status of *visionary* are the ones that embrace and protect their foundational pillars to provide an experience consumers can feel. This commitment flows through the veins of its being, affecting every day-to-day interaction within a brand. Customers can tell when a brand lives up to its foundational pillars, and an authentic foundation can quickly convert consumers to advocates who are the voice for the brand lifestyle and products.

These principles are what make your brand. Start tearing down this foundation and the pillars will collapse, sometimes beyond repair. Be careful in all your decisions, be sure you understand the impact before moving forward, and know the consequences when it comes to your brand's foundational pillars.

Visionary brands hold firm to their principles throughout the best and the worst of times, and that is why they still stand today. It is difficult to build a brand, but even more difficult to maintain and sustain that brand while holding true to your vision—yet that is what is required if you want to create a truly visionary brand.

THE VISION PARADOX

Just because I can SEE . . .

does not mean I have VISION . . .

I have met plenty of leaders who feel they are visionaries. This may be what they think, but in reality, this assumption usually leads their brand to a different conclusion. Unfortunately, having no vision will kill your brand, and thinking you have vision without acting accordingly will do the same.

Being a visionary encompasses many attributes that few actually have been blessed with. Visionaries find ways to balance their long-term vision with short-term wins and present challenges that energize the team. Implementing vision is a constant battle to challenge the status quo and act by intuition where there seems to be no clear path. The impossible is achievable when you have a visionary who refuses to take no for an answer when there is a clear need, even when no solution has been realized.

Henry Ford, the original visionary behind the Ford Motor Company, famously said,

> "If I'd asked customers what they wanted, they would have told me 'a faster horse!'"

This is why visionaries are so few and far between: they are able to see beyond what has already been realized and come up with something that completely revolutionizes how people live their daily lives.

What's more, their vision of the future is not blurred by past successes or failures. Remember, failure is a necessary part of success, and failures are merely a steppingstone to eventually finding a solution. Those who say it can't be done are those who end up missing out on one of the world's great breakthroughs. For visionaries, failures are merely a bump in the road—something they learn from, then move on to conquer the next barrier to achieving success.

I like to look at the context of words and analyze what makes each different from one another. The traditional definition of "vision" describes a characteristic that everyone has. "Visionary," on the other hand, although only three letters different, has a meaning that is 180 degrees removed. With literal vision you anticipate or sense; being a visionary requires being an audacious, impractical risk-taker. This comparison illustrates the quote this chapter opens with about the visionary paradox: just because you have *vision*, that does not mean you are a *visionary*!

The reality of having vision as opposed to being a visionary is that the latter has foresight, and thus can anticipate and clearly define the path forward. Steve Jobs is a great example of a visionary who not only had the foresight but the ability to realize its creation. This is in contrast to a company like Sony: the Walkman was built into a successful product, one that showed vision and was revolutionary in its time, but it was insufficient on its own to carry its success through into the future. Slowly but surely, Sony allowed competitors like Apple to take bites out of a market it once owned and fully realize the long-term potential that it neglected to capitalize on. There are many examples of brands that claim to have vision, but few execute their plan successfully over the long haul.

BREAKAWAY PRODUCT PIPELINE

So if being a visionary is about more than just having vision, just what does someone have to do to be considered visionary? In short, it's about clearing the path—cutting through the fog to realize ongoing innovation through a **breakaway pipeline strategy**. Breakaway products are those that move a brand generations ahead of their competitors, ones that allow them to provide drawdowns in the latter stages of adoption and innovation. It takes the relentless commitment of a visionary to create a product culture of sustained innovation, as well as a company culture of continual execution.

Being able to provide a sustainable pipeline of innovation with market-driving products is a strategy few have mastered, and it inevitably involves many battles on the path to eventual success. A sustainable pipeline of innovation through breakaway ideas is a key principle that determines a brand's long-term fate.

From product drawdowns to adaptable alternatives, there are many reasons the product pipeline is so key for brands to get right. Without an established pipeline culture and strategy, a brand won't get the opportunity to develop the next breakaway product.

Each great breakaway innovation sets the mark and moves the bar higher for the next competitor. Being able to stay ahead is the most important priority for a brand in order to sustain its value with their brand community and retailers while maintaining a competitive advantage. Not only does moving the bar make it more difficult for competitors to overtake them, but it also pushes the brand to always be asking how they can satisfy a need the consumer never knew they had.

The greatest example of a product people never knew they needed—a truly breakaway innovation—was the iPhone. This is a product that was not only built on a solid understanding of how people interact, but redefined communication and interactive culture by itself. The iPhone changed how we communicate and interact on a day-to-day basis, from social engagement to the consumer purchase cycle, loyalty, advertising, value creation, and a slew of other far-reaching areas. Creating as disruptive a product as this took a true visionary to pull off—someone who could not only conceive of the iPhone, but communicate its value to those who may not have understood the reality of how this product was to work in the real world.

In every instance with a breakaway technology or product, it's not just a matter of technological sophistication, but also simple sophistication; the friendlier you can make the user experience (UX), the faster the adoption rate. The end result of investing in a pipeline that focuses on breakaway products is a brand with first-mover advantage, new category leadership, consistent adoption rates, and significant revenue growth.

If managed correctly, this breakaway pipeline can be surfed for many years, even generations. Just make sure never to lose sight of why and what you are putting in the pipeline. Ensure that it is right for the brand and your sustainable vision. It must make sense for the brand and the future of the industry or business.

FORESIGHT

It bears repeating that creating products we never knew we needed requires foresight only visionaries are able to realize. It is always easier to create a better mousetrap instead of revolutionizing the trap itself, although this is not always an easy or safe endeavor to undertake. Safe is risky. The art of "blowing things up" is a very uncomfortable proposition for most companies, and the reason so few are willing to take the risk. But risk-taking is at the heart of foresight, and willingness to take risks is one of the most important attributes a visionary can possess.

When you look at some of the most incredible inventions of our generation, most (if not all) were written off as impossible or even crazy. But it is these crazy inventions that have changed how we live in our world. We should be thankful for those crazies with the foresight and courage to take on the naysayers; if they had not persisted and broken through these so-called impossible barriers, our world would be a much different place.

The visionary understands that progress equals success, and one step at a time, the unachievable becomes achievable. The true visionary with the foresight to know what is needed remains strong in the face of adversity. They need to have the courage to sustain calls to quit or deflect those who say it is impossible. Foresight is a badge of honor—not one to be flaunted, but rather to be used to inspire others to carry the torch in leading others to achieve the impossible.

Hail to those with foresight, for you are the ones who set the future and continue to allow us to live in your vision—now a reality.

REVOLUTION . . . RECREATE . . .

"Incrementalism is innovation's worst enemy."
– Nicolas Negroponte, MIT

Reinvent or Recreate?

Evolution or Revolution?

Innovate or Imitate?

These are choices brands make every day, each representing a safer option or a revolutionary one. Obviously, choosing the more disruptive course will involve a lot of risks, but only by taking risks will you allow your brand to attain a loyal following, leadership position, and sustained long-term revenue growth. Those who are not comfortable taking risks, or do not have the foresight to envision their future, are the ones who struggle to maintain brand equity and loyalty with their core base.

Being able to **out-innovate** yourself first is a key insight from some of the greatest brands on the planet, and the reason they have sustained success over a long period of time. This can be implemented by replacing a product at the peak of its popularity, thereby creating a multi-tier selling opportunity without degrading your brand equity. Or by creating a product so revolutionary it is impracticable for immediate marketplace adoption but leapfrogs you over your competition.

Prioritizing this kind of disruptive innovation platform

requires a **revolutionary mindset**—one that sets you apart even as it defines who you are as a brand. By cultivating this mindset you will be setting yourself apart as a risk-taker and a revolutionary, both of which are common to successful brands. When brands consistently reinvent themselves through their products, it creates marketplace momentum and expectation for the next great generation of innovations.

> "Ideation without realization is just ink—it's not worth the paper it's written on."

Taking pride in who you are and what you stand for is core to most companies, but those who can maintain this flow of innovation and translate it to the marketplace consistently are the ones who are impacting our daily lives.

It takes a revolutionary leader to consistently and passionately drive this process, and that is why again there are so few to emulate. Take heart and learn from these creative, innovative geniuses, for they are the ones who change our world. They are still here, living through their creations in our daily life.

Being revolutionary is a distinction that brings internal rewards and external barriers. This is what drives visionaries and allows them to continue on to the next groundbreaking idea or breakaway innovation, further increasing their lead over those unwilling to risk failure to achieve success.

> "Here's to the crazy ones . . . !"
>
> *– Steve Jobs*

THE ELEMENTS OF A SUCCESSFUL FORMULA

Now that we've taken a look at some of the principal drivers of a visionary brand—breakaway product strategy, loyalty to foundational principles, willingness to take risks, a revolutionary mindset, and others—it's time to translate this into reality. How can you turn your brand into a truly visionary one?

As mentioned above, every successful brand needs to uphold its foundational pillars to ensure ongoing success. More than that, though, you need to follow the formula for success—and like any formula, that requires having the right substances in the right proportions. If you want your brand to become truly visionary, you'll need . . .

- A **creative engine** to support consistent innovation
- Successful **positioning** in the market
- An **omni-channel strategy** to make use of all available means of connection
- A **power triad** that is working in perfect harmony
- Effective use of your **culture matrix**
- A unified **product vision**
- Understanding of your product **ecosystem**
- The **fuel** needed to keep everyone charged and motivated
- A killer user experience (**UX**)
- A strategy to make it in our **new age**
- **Artists** who can bring a human element to your brand
- And the **courage** to stick to your guns no matter the circumstances

While not every brand needs to focus on each of these elements equally, they are a good place to start when building your brand into a visionary company. Each element on its own does not constitute a visionary brand, but keeping a focus on each will move your brand closer to visionary status as a whole. The execution of the formula is difficult, but each provides a building block to your brand, ensuring you can survive the most treacherous storms and thrive on the calm winds.

In the next chapters, we will discuss each step in the formula and how it affects your product, culture, and long-term success. There is a broad spectrum of strategies and elements to building a visionary brand, but collectively they are all crucial to a solid foundational core for the brand to aspire to achieve.

THE CREATIVE ENGINE

"Blow up things that do not work!"

– Tom Peters

The creative engine is where everything starts with a visionary brand. This engine is how you get your great ideas—the breakaway innovations or incremental improvements—to your consumer. It's what sets you apart from the competitors, and it's how you offer tangible points of difference from what is currently on the market.

In commercializing your products you must balance the ability to create synergy between what is right for the brand and what is good for your brand advocates. This is a magical formula that, if mixed correctly, can carry you over generations.

Just don't change the formula once you find something that works! Coca-Cola experimented with updating its formula, and this caused both a backlash with their consumers and degradation of the loyalty they had built over decades. They clearly did not understand that by changing what they had built over the years, they had committed a clear violation of why consumers purchased their products in the first place. Changing the ingredients to iconic products can prove disastrous for brands such as Coca-Cola, Kentucky Fried Chicken, Chick-Fil-A, or any other brand where the formula *is* the brand. Stick with what you know, and what your advocates trust.

These are all examples of brands where the formula is the brand; however, there are also brands that continue to evolve their creative products, processes, and programs. This is what sets them apart, and their formula is the ability for them to translate the culture they are marketing. An example of this are the brands that create an aspirational lifestyle—Nike, Lululemon, adidas, Polo, etc.

This formula analogy can be translated across almost any brand, with the core being an authentication driven by trust through a consistent product, message, and vision. Visionary brands are those that stay true to their central foundational positioning pillars of "What We Make" and "Why We Exist."

Once you have defined your brand formula—what makes your engines roar—it is critical the product foundation is built off this **creative engine** by understanding who you are and staying true to these pillars. Once everyone knows their role in managing the flow, it is critical to not overload the engine with unnecessary hindrances. If you start getting bogged down with the inefficiencies of the day-to-day versus executing your vision, your brand will begin to run like a racehorse instead of a racecar. You will immediately see and feel the difference, and so will your brand advocates. Putting fuel in the engine is not enough; you have to keep fine-tuning the cylinders, the flow of your brand's creative engine to keep it running at its peak performance.

Being able to understand what is needed but not yet invented is creative genius, and it has only been achieved by the few great brands that have maintained a culture that supports this creative engine mindset. It might not be easy, but it's necessary in order to achieve a pipeline of innovative products others envy.

Those driving a brand's creative engine must continue to evolve and revolutionize long-term vision through near-term successes. The road map set by visionary brands may seem short, but it is determined by the long road ahead, not what has been left behind. With that in mind, as we look down the road, we see key components of a successful visionary brand's creative engine: it must be **market-driving**, **disruptive**, and **different**. Each of these qualities by itself has an impact, but when combined they change a product category or disrupt entire industries. An integral part of executing according to these elements of the creative engine is having the foresight to know when you are right and having the passion to work through barriers to achieve eventual success. In other words, you need to know if your creative engine is going to be . . .

MARKET-DRIVING VS. MARKET-DRIVEN

"The only sustainable competitive advantage is out-innovating your competition."

– James Morse

You can either drive your market or be driven by it. It's your choice, but the latter will get you run over by your competition. Whether or not you recognize your competition is coming is not the point; it is whether you have extended your lead far enough where it does not matter what the competition does or does not do.

Being the voice and vision for your category is an enviable position. If you are a **market-driving brand**, one that sets the vision for the market, your competition will inevitably follow you. This is a critical advantage, and one that needs to be hung onto: as soon as you lose your first-mover advantage, it is very difficult to get it back. As soon as you start looking in the rearview mirror you will lose sight of your direction, veer off course, and eventually crash. It's not a matter of *if*, but rather *when* this happens. Recovery may be possible, but you have now given your competition an opportunity to catch up and draft off your momentum. Sustainable brand and/or product evolution is key to ensuring you maintain and grow your lead.

There are many aspects to maintaining your creative engine and positioning your brand, most of which are led by both product creation and strategic marketing. In order to be perceived as the best, you must be understood consistently and authentically to *be* the best. It is the job of the marketing team to bring this product vision to the masses, and more specifically to those brand advocates who will embrace the brand lifestyle and vision. The creative engine will produce the products that put your brand on the road, but marketing will drive the proper messaging. Driving your market requires a consistent flow of imaginative juice, executed through a cohesive team that understands the brand is a living, breathing thing to be nurtured and protected.

Market-driving brands also understand it is not just about product, but rather the entire company at all levels. Operations, logistics, sourcing, production, fulfillment, finance, sales— each plays a part in ensuring that the brand is hitting on all cylinders. Vertical integration of the brand is key to gaining a competitive edge.

As mentioned earlier, if a company fails to bring a great product or market-changing idea to life, the organization suffers the consequences, whether in market share loss, margin decline, or even worse, degradation of loyalty or value perception with your consumers. Each of these eats away at the brand's foundation.

Market-driving brands prevent this erosion and sustain a competitive advantage by having a fiercely competitive attitude. It's important to be protective of the brand foundation and understand what is needed but not yet available as an opportunity to establish a leadership position. This **brand ethos**—the character of your brand, showcasing your relentless competitive personality—can be carried across the entire company, although it also must be continually renewed, refreshed, and authenticated by its visionary, the one who is entrusted with continually energizing the brand both inside and outside.

Credibility is another key driver through both trust and authentication to the outside world. People need to see that what you say is in fact true in your actions, and you need to be authenticating your ethos with those who are part of your foundation. Through creditability and trust, market-driving brands understand the need to ensure these principal elements of a great foundation are continually carried out consistently and authentically. It is through a multi-faceted strategy that brands can sustain growth; the brands that do this are the ones that stay true to who they are and build trust with those who associate with the lifestyle they create.

BE DISRUPTIVE

"Think big; think disruptive. Execute with full passion."
                                                    – *Masayoshi Son*

The word "disruptive" gets thrown around a lot these days, mostly by people who don't really know the context of how it is integrated into companies. Many times, companies try to be disruptive even when it does not make sense to do so . . . or worse, they think they are disruptive when they are not. Either way, being disruptive is an inherent trait shared by visionary brands. Being disruptive involves the ability to create that which has not been created or grab market share from those who are asleep at the wheel.

Disruptiveness is a key principle in a brand's creative engine or arsenal, and most visionary companies are also classic **disruptors**. Being disruptive is what shakes up your industry, makes people look at things differently, or changes the perception of your brand compared to your competitors. Disruptive brands are the ones that aren't satisfied with an evolutionary leap over their competition; rather, they are looking to redefine a market with a generational leap, leading to a new way of interacting or doing business. Disruptors are the ones who are willing to take risks while understanding the potential impact of disruption before executing their plan.

Disruption can take many forms. Among other things, a brand can disrupt through its product, process, technology, or culture. Each of these areas is no more important than the others, but it is how each impacts our day-to-day lives and whether it can be measured through value creation or brand equity enhancement that is important.

When you take a look back, it becomes clear how disruptions have made us more efficient or effective. How we engage with and utilize these market disruptors is a true testament to their impact on our daily lives—think of the Wright brothers, Henry Ford, Thomas Edison, Albert Einstein, Nicola Tesla, John D. Rockefeller, Andrew Carnegie, Steve Jobs, and many others. These market disruptors are few and far between. Their ideas were seen as "crazy" or "impossible" at the time, and each went through significant trials to realize their vision of the future. Even more difficult was getting skeptics to adopt this vision once it was realized. Thankfully, each followed through on their vision and we are all the better for it, having reaped the benefits of progress these market disruptors provide. Here's to the "crazy ones!"

But what does being disruptive mean when it comes to your brand's creative engine? Brands that have disruption as one of their foundational pillars are consistently and continually asking "Why?" Asking this question opens many opportunities to disrupt. It can be asked for any product, process, or technology currently in use, or some idea yet to be realized. Continually asking "Why?" generates those truly revolutionary, breakaway ideas. Once the why has been answered, the next question is "How?" In analyzing great visionary brands, I have found those brands that continually ask these questions and have a clear process to realize the answers are the ones able to build a sustainable flow of innovations, sometimes lasting a lifetime.

But asking questions is not enough. You need to not only have the courage to pursue your vision, but to sustain your brand through the barrage of naysayers and critics you will encounter. Having a great idea is a piece of a much larger puzzle; what you need is the ability to sequentially place the pieces in the correct order at the right time and place. Those who solve the puzzle and can execute their plan into real-life success are generational leaders and true visionaries.

Remember, an idea without a plan is just a dream, and many great ideas lie in the wasteland of broken dreams. Turning a visionary's foresight into concrete success requires understanding how disruptors have succeeded, when to follow a clear path, and when to blaze a new one. There are few "true" disruptors out there, and each one of them had to create a path for us to follow, as each disrupted a market unwilling to either change or understand the vision proposed. More often than not successful brands look to cut their own path as opposed to taking a shortcut to success.

I am not saying that by following the road not taken you are assured success; after all, a cleared path with a defined destination is much easier to traverse than cutting a new path. Remember, it is not an easy journey even when following the trail cleared by these pioneers. This is why being a true disruptor is a treasured title, why so few come along in each generation . . . and why it can be so very beneficial to your creative engine to set disruptiveness at the heart of your foundational pillars.

BE DIFFERENT

"The people who are crazy enough to think they can change the world are the ones who do."

– Steve Jobs

Outcasts are the ones who make an impact on our world. Why is that? Because they are willing to take bold risks and stick their neck out when no one else is willing to do so. It's risky to create something so unique, a game changer that others may not understand. More to the point, it's risky to think differently.

Being different can be categorized according to how people think, act, or learn. Being able to decipher for yourself what is important versus what is not is a gift given to these outcasts, and a platform for those who are willing to look at things differently. Every great visionary or outcast has taken time to stop and ask "Why?"

"Why does this look this way . . . ?"
"Why do we do it this way . . . ?"
"Why is this so hard to understand . . . ?"

"Why" is a simple question, but one with powerful outcomes, and throughout history, the world has changed as a result of being able to answer this question in any area where it is asked. To this day, those who are considered different are still asking this question. Take Elon Musk, the visionary behind Tesla, the electric vehicle standard all are measured against. Faced with naysayers and skeptics, Elon pushed through the BS and found gold where others dared not venture. Thanks to having this mindset and having Elon at the helm since 2008, Tesla is now worth over $658 billion in market cap and has been added to the SP500. Quite a story! But when you have a vision and stick to your strategy, avoid the naysayers and push forward with a team who understands the goal with a passion for the vision, all things are possible.

Having observed many brands over the years, I've found that each has a different way of answering their "Why?" questions, but the common principle between all visionary brands is that the question is asked, and an answer is sought. It is not enough to simply ask the question, but rather seeking an answer that allows you to build a foundation to change the future.

As a case in point: in 1899 the Commissioner of the Patent Trademark Office, Charles H. Duell, was quoted as saying:

"Everything that can be invented has been invented."

Now, while the origin of this quote is disputed, the significance of this idea is obvious. Can you imagine if we would have stopped asking "Why?" in 1899? If we had stopped being disruptive or allowing our creative engines to develop new and different ideas? How dissimilar our world would be!

These outcasts, the different ones shunned from society as crazy—with their different way of thinking, the foresight of these visionaries has given us the ability to revolutionize our way of thinking, ensure progressive development of ideas, and create products that change our lives. Someone willing to be different can have an impact that no one could see coming. Being able to create a vision—and more importantly, to realize it—is one of the most exhilarating feelings one can have over their lifetime.

So the great visionary brands, more often than not, need to have those who are different on their team. They need people who see things not as they are, but as they should be. These are the difference makers who will carve the path to the future and be willing to break down barriers along the way.

Seeing things in a way that others do not and being able to convey this vision to others is a common trait in each of these difference makers. For those who think differently, trying to translate their thoughts into something comprehensible to others seems to be a time-waster, and is counterintuitive, but is a necessary evil on the path to realizing their vision. These geniuses can have a crystal-clear vision, but it is a true difference maker who is able to help others see their idea as something other than blurry or crazy (see the chapter on The Artist below for more on this). Being able to cut through the fog to see the daylight is an enviable position, and should be embraced by those companies that are looking to make a difference in our world.

Let's look at what it means to be different and shake up an established market . . . and what happens when you rest on your laurels and *stop* disrupting.

CASE STUDY: CATEGORY DISRUPTION

How to Disrupt a Market:

1980: Sony introduces the Walkman, a stand-alone product that is immediately considered disruptive by allowing people to disconnect and move with their music.

2001: Apple disrupts the music industry by creating the first true product ecosystem with iTunes and the iPod. With the Walkman as inspiration, Apple quickly picked up market share for portable music players, with the overriding goal of disrupting the music industry by allowing users to download the songs of their choice, giving control back to the user and taking it away from the record industry.

2010: Sony retires the Walkman Cassette after 30 years, having lost substantial market share. Sony sold over 200 million units over 30 years—a success by most standards, but by 2010 it represented a failure to sustain continued innovation. Apple obliterated a product that had not been updated substantially since its introduction.

2010: Apple introduces the sixth-generation iPod Nano. Continuing to implement innovation in technology and miniaturization, the continual product life cycle was perfected by Apple. At the height of popularity, they chose to discontinue and reinvent, creating demand for the next generation while creating brand loyalty for the previous generation.

Being able to create this **product ecosystem** required a vision few had ever thought was possible. It not only connected the dots between disparate products, but also completely changed the way an established multi-billion-dollar industry does business. The transactional, day-to-day operation was completely obliterated by someone who had the vision and foresight to ask "Why?" We'll look more at the example of the Walkman in the "Product Vision" chapter, but for now, suffice to say that the "safe" choice leads only to product extinction.

Instead of falling into that trap, you'll need to take a risk by disrupting the market following this general process:

Market Disruption Process: Innovators Curve

1. Risk versus fear of failure—move on from what has been successful, migrate to a new way of thinking
2. Invent a new solution versus updating the problem
3. Provide what no one knew they needed, and update at peak of demand
4. Disrupt the market and the demand curve:
5. Cannibalize yourself first
6. Simple, sophisticated messaging—personalized
7. Show vision, have courage, and take risks!

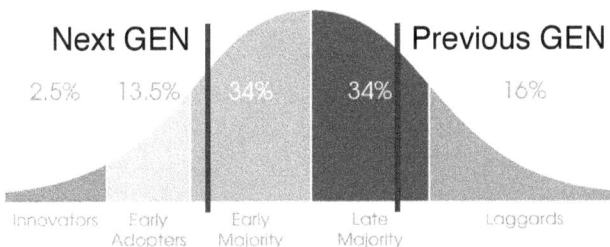

Next GEN | | Previous GEN

2.5%   13.5%   34%   34%   16%

Innovators   Early Adopters   Early Majority   Late Majority   Laggards

Innovators Curve

Visionaries are able to drive through the barriers to success, understand the cultural impact, and turn critics into advocates on the pathway to success as a direct result of their persistent stubbornness and take-no-prisoners attitude. We should embrace their accomplishments, as this assures future visionaries that failure is not final; success is achieved through continually breaking things, always moving forward, and refusing to take a step back just because others have said something was impossible.

This is the creative engine that drives brands to disrupt industries, change how we interact, and punch a hole in the way we feel things should be to achieve how they could be. Build your brand to have a truly disruptive creative engine and you will be all the closer to reaching visionary status.

"True wisdom comes to each of us when we realize how little we understand about life, ourselves, and the world around us . . ."

– Socrates

THE POSITIONING

"Just say NO to COMMODITY!"

– *Tom Peters, The Circle of Innovation*

Brands that are serious about being brands value their equity, as this is the currency of consumer loyalty. Being able to develop an omni-channel strategy, and consistently and cohesively communicate all you do both visually and verbally, will ensure your brand's livelihood over the long term.

At the end of the day, your brand is either premium or a commodity—and it's your choice which one. At the outset of devising your "go to market" plan, one critical area of discussion is your **positioning**. That means answering critical questions such as:

What are we selling?

Who are we selling to?

Where are we selling?

How do we want to be perceived?

Positioning is what determines how you are perceived, and perception is everything. This positioning is critical to the foundation of a visionary brand, as it sets you apart from what you make and how you make it, along with establishing a culture for the brand and how you engage with your advocates.

Prior to the digital age, brands would position themselves through visual imagery and products. This was a static, one-way engagement, and it proved very successful for brands like Nike and adidas, among many others. Now in the age of digital consumer connectivity, with as many as 35 to 40 touchpoints a day and content being consumed 24/7, brands need to be proactive in measuring acquisition cost, and more importantly, ensuring **customer retention**.

The key ingredient in the formula for customer retention is to provide a continual flow of relevant and personalized content on a regular basis. The key here is to ensure each one complements the other, as this provides value to the consumer while building long-term loyalty to the brand.

Interestingly enough, as the amount of digital content that surrounds us increases, our attention span decreases. Flipping the off/on switch has become too easy, and eventually will be automated for us based on very specific personalized preferences. Brands that have not yet adopted a digital strategy that both converts and maintains a connecting point with your consumer through personalization will be the ones left behind by the age of digital transformation.

Just stay true to your foundation as you make use of technology for the betterment of your brand. As is the case with numerous brands that were once classified as premium, it is easy to sell your soul, but impossible to retrieve the positioning you once had. Each brand has a choice; stay consistent, stay true to who you are, and remain relevant to your loyal consumer base. Remember, with our digital lifestyle someone is always watching, and bad news spreads even quicker than before. Keep your brand equity intact by ensuring that your positioning and messaging never go off track. Once your foundation has been fractured, it is difficult if not impossible to repair it.

SELLING YOUR SOUL

Over my years, I have seen many brands that have sold their soul to the devil, and later would try to reclaim their positioning after violating consumer trust. Selling your soul happens when your brand intentionally violates the core foundational principles of the brand ethos. This ethos is what defines you as a brand, and is a tangible connection point for everyone both inside and outside your four walls.

Selling your soul is usually done either due to pressure to hit a number or due to a lack of creativity on how to enter a new market (think of Oakley's struggle as described in the opening chapter of this book). I have seen far too many brands make this mistake. They assume no one is looking, or their transgression is a one-time thing and nobody will notice. But if you know it is wrong, then it *is* wrong. Brands sometimes do not understand it is not only the external customer watching but the internal as well. If there is a disconnect internally, it affects the brand perception externally. Everyone sees everything and selling out is almost never a one-time thing. Like an addiction, the temptation to do it again is strong, and repeated violations weaken and eventually destroy the pillars of brand equity, trust, and culture. If you are not who you say you are visually and verbally, internally and externally, then all becomes blurred in the eyes of your community and brand ethos.

For example: imagine if, say, Apple decided to develop a low-cost cell phone market and began selling cheap, semi-disposable phones at low prices. It doesn't take a huge leap of the imagination to realize how disastrous this would be for their brand equity. Everyone who had bought into the Apple lifestyle would feel betrayed by this change in positioning, as their participation in the brand community would no longer be perceived as a mark of quality or aspiration. And just like that, all the loyalty Apple had built over the previous decades would be irretrievably gone, all for the sake of trying to make a few more dollars. (Note that this is not the same as moving products through a life cycle in a drawdown strategy.)

I'll make it simple: *never* sell your soul to the devil in order to satisfy the needs of the short term. This was something I learned very early on from Jim Jannard, the visionary founder of Oakley. When I was at Oakley heading up the athletic division, Jim would instill into the Oakley tribe his passion for this living and breathing thing he called "Oakley." Oakley was created with a unique, one-of-a-kind culture and image, and everyone inside the corridors of the machine knew what it looked like, how it talked, how competitive it was, and its relentless pursuit to drive the market. Many competitors were left in the dust trying to play catch-up; this is exactly how we wanted to be perceived, and we positioned ourselves accordingly—as the leader, with other brands as the followers. Even beyond the leadership, we had an engrained culture of protecting the brand at all cost, and we stuck together as a family in living up to our ethos. That meant we didn't sell out when the brand hit a challenge; instead we stuck to the vision, and the brand was stronger for it. This dedication came from the fear of losing control to outsiders, being unable to control our destiny. Inevitably many brands succumb to this fear and sell their soul. As a result, the heart and soul of their brand ethos suffer and eventually deteriorate as a result.

Visionary brands hold true to their positioning even though as they grow the market pressure to "sell out" becomes increasingly intense. There is a vast wasteland of brands that have tried to cross this chasm and failed. With the growth of social media, brands must be inherently sensitive to the fact they are being watched by their consumers and brand advocates. The brand that has gained their customers' trust through core foundational values stays true to its positioning, regardless of the temptation, and the visionary brand is the one that passes this test.

Even in hard times, you need to stay true to your foundational principles and what your brand stands for in the marketplace. If you are able to anchor yourself in this foundation, to resist the temptation to sell out for short-term gain, your brand will prosper. Remember, it is not the short term that builds a successful long-term company. Shortsightedness has caused the downfall of many great brands.

On the other side of the spectrum, there are those brands that resisted temptation and were rewarded with increasingly loyal and faithful customers. I have seen brands such as Quiksilver weather the storm of an industry downturn, and instead of panicking in the face of adversity, decided to reward their retailers by being empathetic with them through this period. Many other brands during this same storm decided it was better to survive at whatever cost, including damaging brand equity by abandoning their foundational brand values and positioning. Rather than holding strong through the storm, they found themselves spinning out without any clear direction, and eventually would veer off course and never be seen again. Quiksilver, meanwhile, rode the wave through this storm and came out the back end as the top action sports brand on the planet.

Positioning is a delicate yet integral piece of a brand, as it touches all points both inside and outside a company. Your team and your brand advocates buy into your positioning and brand values and are willing to pay a premium to be part of your future.

BLOODLINES

Central to your positioning are what I call the bloodlines of your brand. The **bloodlines** are the heart and soul of what you stand for as a company. What fills these bloodlines are all your visual and verbal messaging, and according to what you choose to pump through them, these bloodlines can either drain or energize.

What's important when it comes to bloodlines is consistency: ensuring everyone and everything connected with the brand understands what is right or wrong according to your values. This includes not only the employees, but also your brand advocates, as they are your voice to the world.

The other bloodline of brand positioning—beyond being authentic and consistent with your values—is being perceived as **premium**. In order to maximize equity, a brand must earn a consumer's perception of being premium, which is validated by both product performance and the associated lifestyle as a result of using your product or technology.

Premium status is not given; it must be earned, a very difficult task to achieve. Premium status must be carefully managed day to day across all levels of the brand. It must be firmly anchored at the very outset of the brand formation and activated across all aspects of the company. Beyond product (which most people think of when defining a brand), a brand must be premium across all creative and functional levels: design, product creation, operations, logistics, fulfillment, service, packaging, merchandising, etc. It's all good if you're able to provide an insanely great product, but if it's positioned poorly—say, it's packaged as a cheap knockoff, or your brand does not engage with your customer post-purchase—you will not be perceived as premium. This may seem secondary to product performance, but we are living in an experience-driven world, and providing a seamless experience from engagement to purchase to use is a process deployed by all visionary brands.

As I mentioned earlier, you can drive a Lamborghini, but if the engine is not properly tuned it will not run to its fullest potential. The Lamborghini brand is itself a good example of turning a premium product into a premium brand: Lamborghini ensures it exudes the idea of premium at all levels of the company. From pre-purchase through post-purchase, you are not only buying a premium machine, but the heritage and performance of a great, longstanding Italian brand—the bloodlines of a great, visionary brand personified.

Very few have been able to achieve such positioning, and as you can see the product is only one piece of the puzzle. It is what happens behind the scenes prior to a product being released that brings about the magic formula when executed against your brand vision.

THE BEST

> "You do not merely want to be considered the best of the best. You want to be considered the only one who does what you do."
>
> *– Jerry Garcia*

Good, better or best? Every brand enters the funnel into one of these categories, and each category has its distinctive points of difference (PODs). These PODs are defined relative to your product performance and brand positioning.

In its most simplistic form, for those in the "Good" level, their POD is predominantly price point. The "Better" level reflects more of a hybrid POD, with a better product at a mid-tier price point. Then there is "Premium," where you are buying the perceived best-in-class product at the highest category price point. You are buying this product not only for its quality or reputation, but also for what the brand conveys— lifestyle, branding, sponsorships, packaging, merchandising, messaging, etc. These are areas where only a premium brand can play, which drives their strategic competitive advantage.

This is where a brand must be most effective, conveying the brand story and vision to your community. If executed effectively and consistently you will succeed; if not, you will be perceived as another product common to all, special to none. What's more, you will find it hard if not impossible to recover from the misalignment with your brand principles.

The best is perceived when you hit all touchpoints with your consumer: digital engagement, value creation (not just from product, but from the brand itself), consistent product performance, superior fabrication, in-store or online purchase experience, packaging, and yes, the product itself. Each of these investments in the brand experience has a multiplier effect and is an integral touchpoint to your customer; always ensure it stays consistent and authentic. This creates brand loyalty and loops the customer back for additional purchases, community engagement, and a feeling of being part of a global iconic brand. Yes, this is an experience, and most are willing to pay up for such an engagement; thus, the premium badge is realized through the loyalty loop strategy (see below).

Far too many brands overlook the simple things, yet these are what customers find most valuable. Something as simple as quality packaging offers a strategic advantage. Think of how Apple has thought out every interaction in the purchase cycle, with packaging being an experience within itself. What other product can you think of where you actually keep the packaging?

Turning brand experience and customer touchpoints into competitive weapons is an effective strategy. But it's only for those brands that strive to be in the "Best" category.

Create your own distinctive magic and watch how those who engage embrace the smallest subtleties and find this to be a distinctive POD. As with your creative engine, be different in your positioning—in all you do—and people will notice. As you define what best means to you, always understand that you must understand what it means to your potential or current customer. Too many times, brands define who they and what they want to be without an understanding of market perception.

A "Best" level brand can deploy many strategic weapons at every consumer touchpoint. By contrast, a commodity-driven company is forced to compete on a singular point of difference, typically involving lower price point tiered strategies. When you are not a premium brand, you are left with fewer of those PODs at your disposal. This leaves you in a position where you need to defend yourself against competitive price points and value while the premium brands are able to leverage other positioning advantages, both verbal and visual. Believe it or not, providing a superior product with a great buying experience and post-purchase personalized engagement is a rare thing. If executed properly, this "Best" level strategy will allow you to achieve an unbeatable POD beyond just offering a superior product.

When defining your positioning attributes to be the "Best," ensure the user experience (UX) will be a journey your consumers will enjoy. We'll learn more about UX in a later chapter, but for now, remember that an exceptional

UX translates to ongoing consumer loyalty, and "Best" level brands are ones that understand the importance of ensuring this UX is consistently great!

LOYALTY LOOP

As they say, it is always easier to maintain a customer than to attract a new one. This is the principle underlying the strategy known as the **loyalty loop**. In order to sustain your brand revenue and equity, those who purchase from you must be engaged throughout the entire pre- and post-purchase cycle and must be provided an ongoing lifestyle experience.

Prior to the loyalty loop, brands would simply acquire a customer, then move on to the next target consumer without any further engagement. This is now indisputably in the past; the future is built on continual engagement and experience that keeps customers coming back wanting more of the same. Each of these two aspects complements one another, and when exploited together they lead to direct, tangible results in the form of revenue growth, lower acquisition cost, and an increase in brand equity.

Being part of and interacting with a brand beyond just purchasing a product is part of establishing a loyalty loop strategy. No longer are brands disengaging with consumers post-purchase; rather, they are finding this is the time to re-engage and personalize the experience with their consumers. Customers advocating for a brand is a key piece of the branding puzzle for creating and sustaining continual growth of your brand equity.

An example of this new age of engagement is how brands "re-engage" with you post-purchase to buy more products. Most brands will provide current or potential customers with brand or product consideration collateral through different delivery means for review. Once a definitive connecting point is established (click, response, etc.), they will continually and consistently remind you of these consideration points. This can take the form of Google PLAs (product listing ads), product or brand tags, social media targeting, or email campaigns (assuming you have signed up), among many other avenues ultimately culminating in an "add-on" purchase. This is the holy grail for brands, and once achieved you have permission to provide ongoing brand communications and personalized value drivers for your customers.

The main difference between premium and commodity is the strategy developed around personalization of the buying experience itself. Is it obtrusive or inspiring? Is it personalized to my tastes, and does it provide value beyond product? This is the front end of the loyalty loop, and those brands that have mapped this customer journey and personalized the path to purchase are building the first bridge to a successful long-term loyalty loop relationship with your eventual brand advocate.

Premium brands such as Patagonia, The North Face, Mountain Hardwear, Cartier, Tesla, and BMW among others have defined themselves through their positioning, as reinforced through their pre-purchase and post-purchase engagements. With every one of these engagements, they make their valued and loyal customers feel as if they are part of a family and will always be taken care of. By providing this personalized experience, you will find consumers and advocates who also engage in experiences outside of the brand's products. Many times this happens when a cause or event to promote wellness, health, or activity becomes part of the brand itself. Being true to your brand foundation can take many routes, and it is when your customer takes that journey with you that true loyalty to your brand is built.

Personalization is the new age of consumer engagement. The more you are able to fit your product to customers' tastes or activities, the more these customers will advocate for your products and culture, bringing them into the loyalty loop of continued purchasing and advocacy. This loyalty loop strategy is the preferred method for executing your marketing strategy, and ensures your community continues to grow beyond product and begins engaging in your lifestyle. Being able to engage with your consumers and having them proactively promote your brand is critical in the age of digital communications where everyone is connected through dynamic, interactive devices.

Prior to the loyalty loop, brands would take customers through a "Consider, Evaluate, Purchase" cycle, with no back-end engagement. Now, by contrast, we have the opportunity to provide to our loyal customers value beyond initial acquisition, moving to the "Enjoy, Advocate, Bond" cycle. Customers now:

Enjoy your product . . .

Advocate for your brand . . .

and **Bond** with your community.

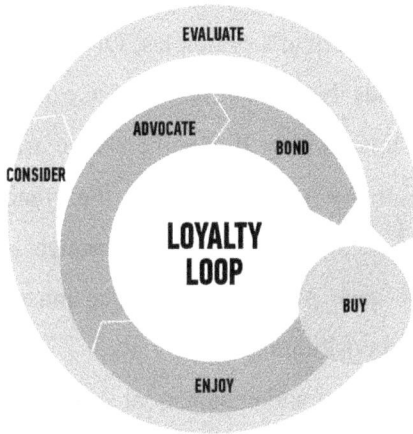

Now, with more tangible tools and metrics, brands are able to change the purchase cycle journey, define purchase metrics, determine priorities, and provide a more personalized post-purchase experience. In other words, we now have the ability to provide value beyond the initial transaction, and the ability to re-engage has fueled the growth of premium brands beyond anything imagined. Moving from consumer "acquisition" to consumer "experience" is what has changed over the decades . . . but as above, sticking to what made you a premium brand must not change as you pursue this strategy.

While all companies can acquire, only premium brands build loyalty through lifestyle engagement. Looking at these segments of the "Loyalty" curve in the graphic above, you can see that all segments are under your control, all are built off your original foundational principles, and all will drive your future if executed well. This is accomplished through direct brand communications, content, engagement, and advocating for the brand's principles. Of course, this can be difficult for brands that are not prepared to execute across the omni-channel touchpoints. Remember, there are many areas in which consumers will engage with the brand during the purchase journey. Whether activating through smartphones, iPads, or PCs, each platform experience must consistently match the brand positioning.

Providing content and engagement that is relevant, to the point, and valuable to your customers is what builds loyalty, and the more personalized the better. This is the power provided by the intersection of technology and digital interconnectivity . . . and it *must* be deployed carefully. While the advantages of technology far outweigh any disadvantages, frequent prompts for engagement still can feel obtrusive to many. In this privacy-first culture, a brand needs to respect the consumer's personal time and choices, as well as being proactive in ensuring they understand the importance of privacy. These values need to be communicated front and center during the engagement phase, as trust is built from initial engagement and nurtured as you move forward.

As mentioned above, many brands end up violating this trust, losing loyalty and diminishing the brand's influence. Needless to say, this can cause significant damage to a premium brand's equity. Post-purchase interactions build a brand's reputation, for better or worse—negative customer engagement can do a great deal of harm, and can end with dissatisfied customers leaving the loyalty loop. Remember, it's called "engagement," not "marriage!" In other words, as hard as you work to bring them into the loop, a customer may quit your brand community for little to no reason and without a moment's thought.

Brands have an opportunity to cut through the clutter, and provide customers with clear, concise, and targeted content strategy. Being able to define what this looks like for your brand is what establishes those who have a visionary mindset versus those who do not. Knowing who you are, what you stand for, and how you are conveying this message connects the dots for your consumers and allows them to embrace your brand culture. The feeling of being part of the brand is a hidden equity few brands enjoy. Visionaries understand this and have a passion for ensuring it never gets lost in translation.

STRATEGIC COMPETITIVENESS

Once you have solidified your positioning at the best, premium level, you are now in a competitive position to solidify market share growth.

Premium brands command the highest margins, have the largest footprint, and provide retailers with leverage to acquire those customers who have an affinity for these rare companies and their products. The strategic advantage is not always in the product, but rather in how it is presented. Merchandising is a key leverage point for premium brands, as they can bring their lifestyle to life in-store and message this to consumers. On the digital e-commerce side, premium brands can also leverage their creative PODs through branding, messaging, sponsorships, or other key lifestyle advantages not offered by commodity companies.

Being in a position to leverage this brand positioning is the ultimate competitive weapon. One area where this strategy is deployed is in the **product squeeze**, where you squeeze a competitor out of a price tier you do not currently dominate. I have seen premium brands that have effectively mastered this weapon to their advantage; Nike and Apple are global, iconic leaders in its execution across all their product categories. In the golf industry, progressive product updates are commonplace; however, it is those who develop an authentically great idea into a breakaway technology that command market share growth.

This was the case with TaylorMade back when they commercialized Moveable Weight Technology (MWT)—a truly authentic breakaway product. With this technology, TaylorMade was able to leverage both the front end of the demand curve—those "early adopters" who absolutely needed the latest and greatest—and the back end, with the "late majority" who had been content with the previous generation of MWT. This was a premium technology that commanded a premium price point and allowed the brand to place products on the front and the back end of the "product squeeze" cycle—helping TaylorMade to significantly gain global market share and authenticate itself further in an industry where this type of product breakthrough is rare.

Once this product strategy had been implemented to rousing success, the only area in which TaylorMade did not command leadership was the mid-tier price point. As we have discussed previously, this is dangerous ground, and you need to tread carefully to make inroads without degrading your brand equity. Ultimately, TaylorMade was able to bridge this gap by reinvigorating a previous brand generation called Burner, which was considered authentic in its day. The strategy was to reinvigorate the Burner label, developing a new, updated generation of products at a mid-tier price point and without MWT. It proved brilliant as retailers and green grass pro shops embraced the strategy, and TaylorMade was able to spread product across all three tiers—Good, Better, and Best. This was only possible through a breakaway technology that was leveraged through progressive updates and new variations of product with differing features from its flagship MWT program.

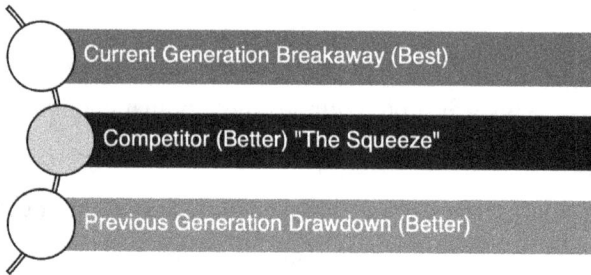

Just as with brands in general, within the consumer products industry there are three traditional category tiers of Good, Better, and Best. Companies that are at entry-level or offer commodity price points are Good; brands that provide more value at a mid-tier price point are Better; and at the top are the Best brands, which have not only established a reputation for superior products, but also have built a loyal following and culture. As above, the entry point to the first tier is price and value, while the other tiers are more engrained with lifestyle attributes, omni-channel focus, and brand equity leverage through ongoing investments in brand activation, awareness, and engagement.

Being there are so few premium brands, retailers will often lock in premium placement for these brands within their stores or online through e-commerce distribution. It is this leverage that allows premium brands to "squeeze" lower-tier suppliers through generational drawdowns. These drawdowns will displace lower-tier brands within the same category, thereby forcing them to either lower their price or be removed from the vendor matrix altogether.

Nike created and positioned the *free shoe* concept to be a combination of casual styling and active use. The idea was to create a shoe someone could wear for running, then be able to walk into a grocery store the same day. Comfort was everything for this user, but so was an authentic product from a brand they trust, and Nike was primed to deliver.

At the time when Nike Free was developed, nothing had crossed the product chasm by blending comfort with performance. Most shoes at the time were overbuilt, bulky, and not comfortable to wear beyond their intended activity. The idea was to blend a shoe anchored in running performance with the comfort to be worn all day. This product created a squeeze effect for Nike; as a result, they obliterated the casual market and reinvigorated the running market with a shoe with performance bloodlines and comfort second to no other brands. As a result of this singular product, the casual performance revolution was born, and today you see similar bloodlines in the athleisure market. Blend performance with comfort and you have an audience ready and willing to purchase.

Just like Nike, find a way to fill a void, one that most people do not realize exists, and you have created a strategic competitive weapon few can or will replicate. Better, even if they do, they will be classified as imitators, not innovators.

This competitive squeeze strategy is launched with current seasonal in-line products, but also through drawdown products, which allow a brand to sell product at lower price point tiers without degrading brand equity. The product squeeze is a brilliant strategy, but it is limited to premium brands and is inaccessible to companies that define price point as their only discernable point of difference. Many brands deploy this strategy, but only a few visionaries have the willpower to stick with their principles while implementing this strategy.

Some brands have offered lower price point products or distributed to lower-end retailers in an attempt to deploy a product squeeze, and they found themselves in repair mode as a result. In our economy today it is best to assume someone is always watching, and this holds true especially for premium visionary brands. Premium brands need to strike a delicate balance between a successful product squeeze and being perceived as only selling a commodity.

Having seen the product squeeze strategy deployed firsthand, I believe it is a primary reason many premium brands establish significant market share growth in their respective categories. Many of these brands (e.g., The North Face, Nike, adidas, Oakley, Callaway, Cole Haan) are ones you purchase every day, not so much based on value, but rather on brand perception and positioning.

PROMOTE A LIFESTYLE

Everyone sells products; brands sell lifestyles. Ralph Lauren famously once said, "We are selling a lifestyle, not a product."

In order to execute this, just be sure to have a strategy built around consistently selling this lifestyle to your consumer.

Visionary brands understand their product is a culmination of proper positioning and a sustained commitment to their brand principles. Being able to promote this product as a **lifestyle experience** is a strategy unique to premium brands and not shared with those classified as commodities.

This can be conveyed through both visual imagery and verbal connection with your consumer. Your community needs to feel as if they are part of your lifestyle as soon as they purchase. You will find the brands that deploy this positioning strategy are ones that connect the dots for consumers. Living each day passionately is a common aspirational goal for all customers, and your ability to include this aspiration in your vision and help your customers connect their life and their family to your brand is truly what will set you apart.

The opposite of this strategy are brands that position themselves only through industry terminology and detailed product specifications, with no human thought or physical touchpoint being thought out. Predominantly these are commodity brands looking to provide a price-driven point of difference, as opposed to a lifestyle impact. Having this strategy is not necessarily wrong, but its limited impact is apparent by asking one simple question:

**How do you connect with your consumer
in a personal way?**

It is not through impersonal or technical messaging; it is done by embracing their lifestyle and providing tools to make it more enjoyable. Choose to personalize, be authentic, and embrace their lifestyle by conveying the lifestyle associated with your brand.

Lifestyle promotion is a clear point of difference for a premium company and why a consumer is willing to pay a higher price point for a product with similar functional attributes but drastically different lifestyle or culture positioning. Again, this is why visionary brands are so committed to securing their identity, continually reminding potential consumers of the attributes realized when they join the brand community. This is a strategy that stays consistent and cohesive across channels, both online and in-store.

A sustained lifestyle message with premium product alignment, consistently carried across multiple consumer touchpoints, is a powerful combination. Stay away from the bloody, shark-infested waters of commodity products; rather, enjoy the open ocean opportunities of premium products and lifestyle where your target consumer swims. Accommodate their desires beyond product and make them feel special. While commodity brands haggle over price, premium visionary brands look to bring consumers value and an aspirational lifestyle experience to each engagement with their community.

Being able to recognize and capitalize on this open ocean strategy is where visionary brands set the standard for the rest of the world. Being able to create a new opportunity with a current segment of business by design realizes new opportunities for everyone. If messaged properly and the overall commercialization strategy is executed properly, you will gain first-mover advantage, the respect of your competitors, and the loyalty of your customers. Sustaining this competitive advantage will allow you to ride this wave until you create the next, even bigger wave to jump on. This is very difficult if not impossible unless you have a culture built around a commitment to experiment, fail, create, and succeed (see the Culture Matrix chapter).

Strategically competitive positioning for all visionary brands starts on day one, before the company is ever conceived. It is accomplished by defining the brand's foundation and building a structure that can stand a lifetime. The brands that have established a vision of what will be in the eye of their consumer and never lose sight of what made them in the first place are positioned to ensure this image always stays intact.

THE OMNI-CHANNEL STRATEGY

Your **omni-channel strategy** represents consistent, value-driven communications throughout all aspects of your brand's purchase and engagement cycles. It is a key part of your formula for long-term success.

A great example of this strategy successfully executed comes from adidas. As a brand, adidas engages with their potential customer long before a purchase is made. Most of these engagements are in the form of messaging designed to help that potential consumer become part of their aspirational lifestyle community. The brand effectively engages before, during, and after a purchase, providing value beyond purchase and building a loyal community of brand advocates. The key is to continue engaging, personalize the messaging, and provide ongoing value.

The omni-channel strategy has evolved over time, and only recently has it involved tying together dynamic digital tools to ensure a brand continues to drive consumer loyalty, brand equity, and long-term revenue. These ingredients are integral to a brand and are the lifeblood of engaging loyal consumers consistently and effectively with your products and lifestyle.

The combination of brand value, lifestyle engagement, and generational products is a winning formula few have been able to consistently achieve. What's more, mapping this combination effectively across all engagement platforms is very difficult to execute. With a vertical multi-channel execution, brands ensure there is no disconnect between positioning and product. The ones that successfully navigate the elements of this formula will solidify their future, with a clear vision and path for others within the organization to follow and for your competitors to envy.

The customer journey is significantly different from even a few years ago, as tech and "Big Data" have evolved more rapidly than we could ever have imagined. The engines of an omni-channel strategy are the keys that unlock success . . . or chaos:

Striking a balance among all these different facets is very hard to achieve, and very easy to break once established. Once you have set your path, be sure to learn along the way and adapt aggressively in order to solidify your leadership position. Gauge previous results, which ultimately should allow for creating a better path forward and an improved UX. This is the circle of life for a brand, and while these engines independently may not drive a brand far, collectively they are unstoppable when executed properly.

Most brands that have successfully defined, communicated, and integrated their omni-channel strategy embed their strategy at all levels of the organization. This provides clear guidelines and expectations for both employees and consumers, which can be encapsulated in this optimal omni-channel equation:

Employees know what is right for the brand, while consumers know what to expect from the brand.

When either side of this equation is disrupted, it is usually through a breakdown of one of the omni-channel components. For example, launching a new product without including options for personalization degrades the entire brand experience. Whether this breakdown is small or large, addressing it is an integral piece of ensuring the brand continues to thrive from the inside out.

Brands have a distinct competitive point of difference if they can bridge the different components of an omni-channel experience. There are many areas where this execution can be ineffective or clog up the pipes, slowing the efficiency. All components need to flow smoothly for faster product commercialization, efficient communications, consistent communications, and personalized buying experiences that allow for a closed loyalty loop experience. The more efficient the product commercialization, fulfillment, and buying life cycle experience, the more tangible the ROI and the more profitable a company becomes over the long term.

So many companies are adopting this omni-channel experience due to the changing face of retail. Brands are now more in control of their own destiny and are investing in their own success instead of the retailers'. This is a classic changing of the guard, with a majority of revenue still being generated by classic "brick and mortar" retail stores, but the future of retail holds a much different fate. As a result, brands must be sensitive to the appropriate allocation of spending with these key retailers versus internal brand investment. Either way, omni-channel is key to ensuring you have an exceptional brand experience across each distribution channel. This is the beauty of investing in your future: both the brand and retailer benefit, and the brand is better prepared for where the market is eventually going. Blending the mix—proactively updating ongoing omni-channel investment relative to the revenue demand shift of store versus direct-to-consumer (DTC) sales—is a tactic most brands will need to manage as part of their key performance indicators (KPIs).

Each brand that is managing this channel matrix is different from the others, and their respective success or failure comes down to being progressive or regressive. Some are paralyzed by the fear of the unknown, while others have a clear-cut path through the darkness. The old adage from Ben Franklin offers some wisdom:

"By failing to prepare, you are preparing to fail."

Moving ahead with a well-thought-out omni-channel plan with proper allocation of resources and ongoing multi-functional support will surely put you ahead of those who have not yet taken any steps towards implementing a strategy. The easier the process of interacting with your brand is, the greater lifetime value you create with your consumer.

This is a formula most visionary brands have adopted. Omni-channel is a living, breathing thing, and is constantly evolving. Each brand faces the difficult task of staying ahead of consumer demand and ensuring they are providing unique, personalized value for their consumers' time. Time is money, money is time; both are important, so recognize what you need to do in order to execute on both. This evolutionary process is similar to that faced by the computer industry at its outset, though perhaps it is moving at a faster velocity than processor speeds. That is, as consumers we are not necessarily asking for increased speed (but will take it when it is available!), but we *are* demanding faster fulfillment every day. This is satisfied by successful brands that dynamically execute an omni-channel strategy.

In an earlier chapter, we looked at how disruption can be a force for good. So when considering your omni-channel strategy, it may be time to ask:

How do we disrupt current industry norms?

Visionary brands are constantly asking this question, leading to breakthroughs that change an industry. Having disruptors as part of your overall strategy process and helping to integrate ideas at all levels of the omni-channel experience is a key weapon for those brands daring enough to proactively embrace these "crazy ones." This is easier said than done; you must have committed leadership from the top down, and you need someone who understands the implications of the vision in order to translate it to the masses.

This is where innovation is bred, adopted, and executed. Execution can take many forms and is where many brands derail—it's not that their systems and resources are wrong, but rather, they tend to take shortcuts through the path of least resistance. Execution with your omni-channel strategy requires the collective work of everyone associated with the brand. This is a path where most brands end up going off track and do not stay committed to building brand loyalty and trust with customers. This is a delicate balance to strike.

Let's take a look at an example of not executing on your strategy. Imagine you have received a product that exceeds your expectations—fit, form, and function are all great—but come to find out the value proposition beyond product is secondary and not well thought out. In this instance, a brand that conveyed a lifestyle had products to match but was not committed to executing the experience for its customers.

If your competitive edge is authenticity within the field of road or mountain biking, and you provide products that fit with this image, make sure you are providing the same value and experience to your loyal advocates. Those voices are a powerful barometer as to the ongoing experience consumers have with your brand. For better or worse, make sure you have a plan to ensure consumers buy what you are selling, both product and lifestyle.

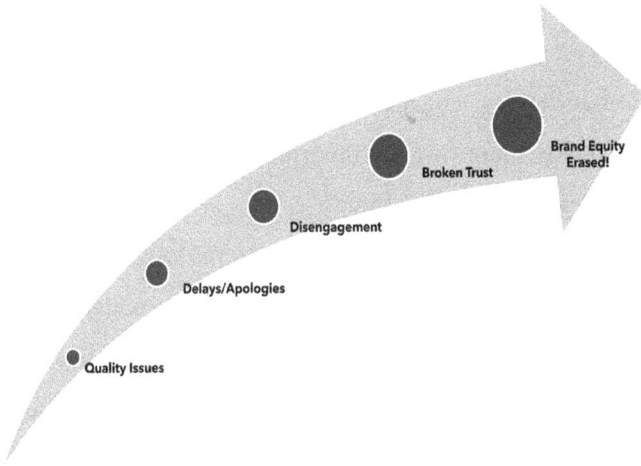

Brand Equity Erased!

Broken Trust

Disengagement

Delays/Apologies

Quality Issues

The Trust Factor

Each of these trust detours can be difficult, long, and arduous to overcome. Most brands recover from setbacks like this, but some will wither and die. Even those that weather this storm are usually weaker for it, and are vulnerable to competitors. Being able to manage ongoing development of your omni-channel strategy and execution is integral to growing and maintaining your status as a visionary brand and ensuring you are managing expectations both internally and externally.

When companies think of omni-channel, they reference cohesiveness in their distribution channels and simplicity in acquiring their products. This is certainly an important aspect of omni-channel, but true visionary brands think of **vertical omni-positioning**, meaning being vertical with no disconnect either inside or outside the brand. This means being vertical in *all* you do—messaging, positioning, marketing, product, customer service, engagement, and UX execution. Each of these builds upon one another, and as a whole, the brand becomes an unstoppable force.

Being able to sustain this vision over the long term requires a vertical omni-positioning vision, one easily understood by your advocates outside the brand and passionately embraced by all inside the company. There is always a reason someone joins your team, and many times it is the vision you have set for the future, not the paycheck. This brand "juice" is what fuels these employees, and why being vertical in all aspects of the brand evolution across all functional areas is so crucial to the brand's livelihood and development of its culture (see "Fuel" for more on this topic).

Visionary brands stay true to who they are, build themselves around a lifestyle persona or experience, passionately embrace the principles of the brand, and consistently inject these values into their team each and every day. Passion wears thin when you no longer understand what you stand for, or when you do not have a visionary consistently ensuring this messaging is flowing throughout the bloodlines of the company.

The company is the brand, the brand is the product, the team is the brand *and* the product. Stay true to your vision in whatever you do, from the top down and bottom up.

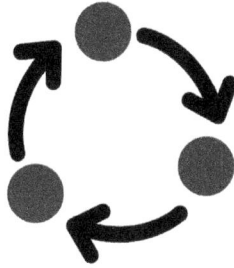

THE POWER TRIAD

Brand visionaries are the ones who drive the company forward, allowing for distinct, definable points of difference from their competitors. They know what their long-term vision is and how they are going to get there, ensuring they are proactively managing and integrating teams across all functional areas of the brand. Most importantly, they do not look in the rearview mirror, are not concerned with what their competitors are doing, and are always looking for ways to drive their market forward. This is called a first-mover advantage strategy and is predominantly led by the product team.

However, in order to drive the market forward through product or channel disruption, you need a team to bring it to market and successfully sell it. The team at the heart of your vision is the **Power Triad**: three functional teams tightly woven together, yet independently managing their own parts to continually build, message, and sell products to your brand advocates. The power triad is an interdependent leadership team that builds the future of the brand, ensures its products are revolutionary, and continually drives the foundational principles of the brand forward.

Product

Sales

Marketing

These independent and interdependent functional teams are the ones that assure all cylinders are firing within the brand. The brand machine requires multiple teams to drive it, and for a visionary brand's needs, one team must be taking the lead while the others contribute to the successful commercialization of these ideas, assuring they are successfully translated and sold to the retail marketplace. This leader for our purposes is the *product* team; they must be the visionaries behind every great idea, while the *marketing* and *sales* leaders play an integral role in the positioning, marketability, and acceptance of each new creation.

Let's take a closer look at one side of the triad. The marketing team is part of the creation process from the outset, being briefed on the idea strategy, competitive POD, product commercialization plan, and positioning. This team has input on the front end and follows the process through commercialization. They do not wait for the product to be commercialized, but rather are proactively developing a cohesive brand strategy for the launch, preparing to show it off to the world while the product team moves closer to unveiling the new creation.

The interesting part as you move along in this process is the anticipation for the next generation of products is tangible for those with your brand, and even more for those outside the brand. Most visionary brands with product category leadership will find themselves continually building a community loyal to any new creation or product update they may bring to life. This is the case whether selling apparel, footwear, cars, tech, services, or software—all have a loyal following as a result of their positioning and unconditional focus on the brand's foundational principles.

Relative to how quickly this release process happens, brands are able to create demand across the entire adoption curve, and by design increase demand while decreasing inventory and maintaining brand equity. By expediting technology, commercialization, or design you can increase adoption rates, all while continuing to squeeze (see "product squeeze" in the Positioning chapter) the competition and maintaining your category margins.

This makes a great formula for success, but is not possible without a cohesive, collaborative power triad creating a pipeline of great ideas, innovations, and commercially viable products. Bringing products from a mere idea to reality is the role of the product team's creative engine, but bringing it to life to the outside world is the role of marketing. It is in marketing's hands to translate the product POD, user experience, and positioning within the brand's ecosystem of products. Any disconnect among these areas is deadly for the longevity of the brand. Remember, it has to make sense for the brand, and it is the visionary brand's role to figure out what is right for their loyal community, perhaps creating something they never knew they actually needed.

Bringing insanely great ideas into the real world, as is the case with Apple, is what separates visionary brands from the rest, and with a solid power triad in place, these ideas can be realized. Each idea that comes through the innovation pipeline must be clearly defined through market opportunities, brand synergy, and channel positioning, and ideally should be integrated with the current ecosystem of products.

Market-driving creations are often first thought of as "impractical" or "irrational." It is up to the visionaries in your power triad to convey the practical side of an otherwise impractical product.

This was the case with the light bulb; Thomas Edison has been referred to as the "father of invention," demonstrated by his filing over 1,093 patents, many of which were for innovative, breakaway products we still use today in some form or another. Edison's idea for an improved light bulb was shunned by most: a British Parliament committee indicated Edison's light bulb was "good enough for our Transatlantic friends, but unworthy of the attention of practical or scientific men." In the same context, a British Post Office engineer said that the "subdivision of the electric light is an absolute *ignis fatuus.*" In other words, a dream never to be realized. The results of Edison's dedication should be obvious to anyone alive today.

Another example of a product that was dismissed as impractical was the laptop computer. We certainly could not imagine life without the indispensable laptop computer, but laptops were initially written off due to their structural issues, battery life, and high price. All of these issues at the time would quickly be resolved through the rapid evolution of printed circuit board miniaturization, processing power improvement, and battery life performance. But even as recently as 1985 *The New York Times* had written off laptops, indicating they were on their way out!

Who could have imagined the impact an idea like a light bulb or laptop computer would have on our daily lives? And all thanks to those translators of great ideas, the marketers— who, in alignment with the product team, were able to translate their vision. That's just what a power triad is capable of: translating that which seems impractical to others, but is needed by all, and incorporating a breakaway technology into a product no one knew they needed. The power triad is the team that defines our future, realizing our dream through passionate creation.

On the front end of this ideation process, the product and marketing teams are responsible for flushing out ideas and finding those ideas that the product team can adapt, recreate, or blow up to find the future opportunities that are best moved into the pipeline.

Each member of the power triad team needs to be in sync with one another and very respectful of one another's space. This space and the syncing process among the three teams is inevitably what sets the foundation for a truly visionary brand. Not being able to manage the power triad or to understand the weight it carries in defining a brand's existence is an area where most brands fail. Leaders of brands are inherently reluctant to take risks, and most talk the talk, but few walk the walk and actually follow a new path to successful disruption. Based on that resistance to risk, too many brands meet their power triad with continual resistance, which is why there are so few brands that are able to sustain long-term growth.

The system is the process, the process is the system, and the power triad defines the execution of each. Much like a franchise operation, once a system is in place and it works, the burger gets cooked the same way each and every time—this is why it's so important to support your power triad for long-term success right from the outset. Embrace failure and cheer success.

In order to build a long-term sustainable flow of ideas, there must be a process that allows for creative independence as well as the interdependence among the power triad teams to assure each product eventually is brought to market or removed from the process if it is not determined to be right for the brand or its consumers. This interdependence among the power triad teams is integral to ensuring a continual flow of ideas that are both practical and revolutionary. An idea is only an idea unless it is eventually brought to market; not all ideas are great ideas, and this is yet another reason the power triad process is so important to assure there is a "flushing" process to idea flow.

The objective of the product team is to keep the brand (and not your competition) moving forward, exceeding expectations and always driving the market instead of being driven by it. The objective of the rest of the power triad is to build a story around these great ideas, defining their competitive advantages and unique POD and providing the story to tell the world. This seems logical, but many companies or brands do not understand this simple principle and flow of ideas. Independence without interdependence equals failure.

Let's take a look at what an inadequately supported power triad might look like. While bringing its football cleat to market, Under Armour was able to gain significant market share within the category over a short period of time. They had anchored themselves in authentic product positioning, reinforced with great marketing. However, the product was released too soon, and unfortunately, it became the victim of ongoing quality issues. Clearly, this was a case of putting marketing ahead of product and releasing a product that was not ready for primetime. Fortunately, Under Armour was able to rectify the problems, but not without pulling product from the shelves and righting the ship. This was the right move, and they have since gone on to overwhelming success in the category, although they lost a great deal of goodwill and trust in the process.

Unfortunately, I have seen many brands try to bring a product to market before it was ready. This happens when marketing jumps ahead of the product team and brings it to market too soon. This is a deadly recipe for failure— not only for the product, but also for the brand. When this short-circuiting happens, it almost always results in trust being broken with the end users, and thus with the brand advocates. Either a product fails to meet expectations or does not perform as promised. I say "promised" in this instance as the issue typically is not with the product, but rather with the marketing proposition. I have unfortunately seen many consumer brands follow this disastrous path to meet a deadline, retailer expectation, or some other poor reason only to end up degrading the brand. As with other disasters, this is a slow, painful learning process. In contrast, if a leader follows a continual, repetitive, consistent process with their power triad team, most if not all of these types of self-inflicted disasters can be avoided. Having these teams in sync with one another, along with having direct, consistent communication, will ensure this breakdown does not happen.

Now, there will be circumstances beyond your control where the timing is not working in your favor, but you must remain flexible and adjust. Be pliable; just do not tear apart. Times of crisis are when a person's character is tested and their ability to be a leader is challenged. The best remedy for any situation is communicating, educating, and remaining calm. And there remains one constant throughout this scenario: DO NOT break the power triad process flow. In breaking this chain, you will inevitably pay the price somewhere along the distribution chain, whether through your customer, community, or retailer.

This may be easier said than done, as many global brands have broken this chain. Some survived, but many never recover their premium status. Being committed to foundational principles is similar to building a house on a rock-solid foundation versus one of sand—one that is solid during storms, not one that sinks. Being able to withstand the temptation to speed up or rearrange the power triad's process is key—just DON'T do it. You will be the better for it in the long run.

Visionary brands will always have a vision of what is right for the brand: proactively embracing disruption, consistently translating the vision, and effectively engaging with their brand advocates.

Great Product + Great Marketing = SUCCESS

Bad Product + Great Marketing = FAILURE

Your power triad can either break out or break down, according to your leadership. You must be committed to a process flow for realizing your dream of building, creating, and bringing to market products that disrupt the status quo, breaking things that are illogical or simply do not work.

Breakout

- Each needs one another
- Follow triad cycle flow
- Interdependent

Breakdown

- Each needs itself only
- Follow single cycle flow
- Independent

This system of breaking things provides power to the triad and is critical to assuring you do it in the best, most efficient way. It is a way to ensure those who are part of your brand bloodlines—including your team and your brand advocates— know what to expect in your process. By having a commitment to this process, some of the greatest innovators will gravitate to your brand, as they know by your actions what you stand for and how you stand by them . . . your foundation.

Putting aside their later problems (which they recovered from successfully, as it happens), I was fortunate to be with Oakley during a period of driving chaotic, disruptive, innovative products and teams. We were relentless at defining the market—always disrupting, creating and exploiting a first-mover advantage, and having the attitude of wanting to show the planet how insanely great our brand was without fearing failure or our competition. This is what a disruptive power triad looks like in action, and it will serve you well if you are committed to nurturing and supporting its evolution and growth.

Those leaders who understand you must be different to stand out are the ones who will fail the most, but also succeed the longest. Hail to those willing to take the lead in providing an avenue for those innovators to create a voice for the next generation!

THE CULTURE MATRIX

"Nearly all people can stand adversity, but if you want to test a person's character, give them power."

– Abraham Lincoln

The **culture** of the brand can be defined as its core principles and values. These are ingrained inside of the corridors of the brand and embraced by those working for it. If a brand has not yet defined these values and principles or defined what it stands for, then it is merely a company selling a product.

A core foundational principle of a brand is how it defines and develops its culture—what it stands for, and the actions that flow through its bloodlines to consistently and authentically communicate this culture to those inside and outside the brand. The bloodlines of the brand are those who work to carry out these actions, and a brand must be consistent in all that is communicated both visually and verbally. More than that, the passion for a brand *is* its culture: when you have clearly defined what you stand for and who you are as a brand, it is easy for those in your bloodlines to have a passion for feeding and defending the brand's foundation. This is core to why some companies thrive while others suffer sustained employee turnover and barriers to growth.

In some cases, the culture of a brand can be so thoroughly embraced that it seems almost cult-like in the degree to which they defend its values, principles, and products. I use the term "**culture matrix**" to define this phenomenon that to others can seem intangible. The tangible nature of this brand positioning is the story effectively told through every communication, product, or process. I find this matrix intriguing, as it seems to engage with those who feel like a part of the brand through tangible and intangible means—those who are a part of the community. When the brand is connecting directly with their needs through its products, this is when it becomes consistently tangible and the connection becomes reality.

There are four distinct areas a brand must focus on continually in order to build their culture matrix:

1. Authentication: be authentic in ALL you do, say, and feel. Yes, emotions can get the best of people; ensure everyone understands what you stand for and why you exist.

2. Character: character flaws have brought down many brands. These can be flaws with culture, communications, or engagement, or other direct verbal or visual interactions. Stay true to who you are, and you will not have to apologize for a disconnect in character.

3. Loyalty: be loyal to those who purchase, engage with, and interact with your brand. Bring the loyalty loop home and make them feel special. Personalize everything.

4. Trust: be trustworthy. Be a brand others respect not for products, but for who you are and what you consistently stand for in the world.

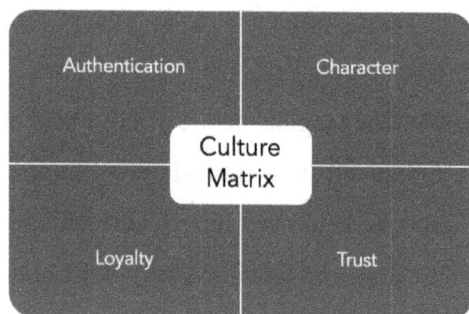

Defining your brand culture allows those on the outside looking in to gravitate towards your values, as a result directly influencing a team of passionate cultural advocates. The culture matrix continues to grow and be defined through this interactive anchoring of values and principles.

Where some companies believe they are brands, the external reality is much different in the absence of an authentic brand culture. Culture breeds stickiness among advocates, and perception becomes reality. You cannot say you are a brand when you have not proactively managed to define your core identity. This clearly defined identity is a key component of your brand culture and bloodlines. In most instances, brands become brands as a direct result of what they are selling— in the case of most successful brands, a lifestyle. Premium brands' defined POD comes from their product and premium positioning. This premium positioning is in itself a component of a brand's culture, as it conveys a lifestyle enjoyed by those who embrace the lifestyle experience the brand is selling.

Think of premium brands like Ralph Lauren, BMW, Porsche, or Lamborghini. As described in the chapter on Positioning, these brands sell a lifestyle as much as their products, and while these products command a premium price point, those purchasing the products have high expectations for performance as well. Culturally these brands have inherently positioned themselves in this premium product tier in order to both differentiate and exclude them from knockoffs. This claim to a premium brand culture is rightly earned by those who are part of the brand driving the culture, who have an ongoing obligation to ensure brand value and positioning are consistently followed.

If there is any disconnect between the brand vision and reality, those inside and outside of the brand who carry the foundational torch will quickly look to correct any misalignment. (It's worth noting that *torchbearers* are those who evangelize for your brand vision within your brand, while *brand advocates* exist outside your brand's four walls.)

These brand torchbearers have an immense responsibility, but if the foundational principles are understood by all, then there should be no disconnect. No disconnect, and a clear connection to the outside world.

In contrast, I feel the foundation of a brand can and should be challenged at times, for a brand without a solid core foundation will not withstand these challenges. These challenges can come in the form of brand communications, customer service, product issues, or some other ethical quandaries. The way a brand approaches these challenges needs to fit with its culture and foundational principles. It is crucial that challenges be taken head-on, but the foundation must always stand.

When you have an effective and efficient power triad flow, along with these strong foundational values supported by the brand's culture, you will have a brand that can withstand the storms in good times and bad. Very few can make this claim, and this is another key to realizing a truly visionary brand status.

"I believe in the power of a positive, high-performance culture, which begins with strong ethical values at the core."

– Ron Williams

CULTURE AND LEADERSHIP

Ethical brands have a culture of creating a singular voice consistent with a clearly defined set of brand values and principles. I say "singular" as this voice needs to be communicating a cohesive message. Your culture is defined by the tangible applications of what the brand stands for, and it is established through consistent action.

Companies often face culture issues related to these foundational principles: when their principles are not clearly defined, their messaging and commitment become muted as well. This is when brands can run into trust problems or ethical issues, leaving them without a clear path through a potential storm. Having a clearly understandable, highly ingrained culture matrix—one that is defined by who you are and what you stand for, and is anchored in your core foundational principles—will provide clear direction through any storm.

One area where brands have found cohesive cultural leadership is through servant leadership. **Servant leadership** realized through an authentic, ethical foundation of brand values is a key component to providing culture growth that becomes ingrained throughout the entire company. This refers to the actual tangible feeling of giving back or providing service to others in need. This can be manifested in a brand's culture through creating programs that inherently reflect the commitment to a lifestyle promoted by the brand itself, or supporting those inside the brand to achieve and grow in their roles.

One such company that is committed to servant leadership, proactively embraced from the top down, is Patagonia. It takes not only consistent commitment, but also a driving force from those at the helm of the company. Patagonia's cause-driven focus on environmental protection is framed in this way:

"Patagonia supports environmental organizations with bold, direct-action agendas and a commitment to long-term change."

What a great anchoring statement for a company committed to servant leadership! This mission statement epitomizes truly, authentically making our world a better place for us and future generations. This by design ties directly to the lifestyle Patagonia, its employees, and its loyal tribe of customers are committed to on a daily basis. Who would not be energized by hearing and seeing this messaging promoting inside the four walls of the brand you passionately support?

Those brands that have positioned themselves through serving a cause or others must understand their goals and the impact of their service. This is a selfless objective, and one that warrants praise if followed through as planned. Everyone inside an organization with a culture of servant leadership should feel empowered to proactively serve others with knowledge, patience, and guidance; this is what creates a cohesive culture, one built on assisting each other and the brand, not winning individual accolades while stomping on others. If this value is part of your brand, be true to it, drive it into your culture, and ensure all who provide this service are recognized and, where needed, rewarded.

At its core, servant leadership can be accomplished wherever there is an alignment with brand values and the ability to provide a service for the betterment of your employees, customers, and causes on a global scale. I found that those visionary brands that adopt a culture of servant leadership have an additional POD over their competitors, and are better able to hire the best talent, as their values come through more authentically as a result. Those who join brands are oftentimes looking for principle-centered values ingrained in the company, a place where they can provide a benefit to others at work and outside of work. Always keep it real, and ensure others understand the importance of this principle. It is better to give with no expectation of return—this is the anchor of servant leadership.

But there are certainly other manifestations of culture. Not every brand can effectively implement servant leadership, but all culture needs to be driven by **character**. Culture that exists without character is neither authentic nor tangible. Let's look at how character-driven leadership affects a few other aspects of the culture matrix.

First, there's **foundational character leadership**. When developing a culture, your brand's character needs to be reflected at all levels of the brand, echoing continually through the corridors of the organization. Character is proven when it is conveyed consistently in what you say or do inside and outside of your company. This may seem easy to achieve, but it the difference between building a house on a faulty foundation—hard to build, easy to break—as opposed to a rock-solid foundation where the forces of nature cannot destroy it.

Are you building your character on a weak foundation, or a rock-solid one? Is the house you built easily destroyed, or can it withstand the onslaught of internal and external forces looking to destroy what you have created? Your foundation is built on several principles, but character, both personal and professional, is a key pillar to ensuring you can withstand the stress and strain of everyday life. Trust can be destroyed through misalignment of brand values or built by keeping true to your foundational character.

Diversity and **values leadership** are two branches extending from foundational character in your culture matrix. A diverse culture is a healthy culture—one that embraces differences, embraces a different way, embraces challenges, and encourages breaking things to drive the brand forward. People have a tendency to pigeonhole diversity without embracing the significance it can have for all areas of a brand's cultural foundation. Diversity can change the world, our way of thinking, our way of interacting with others, and providing a values-driven leadership model can have a trickle-down effect across the company.

Culturally, I would say this values-driven leadership is where most visionary brands lose their foothold on the brand, their team, and their brand advocates. When leadership fails to maintain the brand's culture of values, trust is broken and is difficult to repair. This is a very delicate balancing act, and one not to take lightly. Leadership must be held accountable for both creating and sustaining a culture in which foundational principles-centered values are at the core of business decisions. This can be broken at differing levels within the organization, but it is incumbent upon these leaders to ensure when this disconnect happens it is quickly affirmed that this does not follow the brand's overall core values. Too many leaders water down their commitment to cultural principles, which leads to that brand not being considered honest or sincere. And true sincerity is not coachable; it is ingrained in those who believe in what they are saying and ultimately doing.

To say and not do leads to a weak foundation. To say *and* to do is a strong foundation and will withstand any disruption. Living up to their cultural values is a choice visionary companies make every day. In fact, the choice to anchor your brand to a principle-centered culture is a common theme with all visionary brands I have been a part of throughout my years.

While at Oakley, prior to the Luxottica acquisition, we had a very take-no-prisoners approach to our culture. This culture was embraced by the whole team, and it was continually reinforced with us on a daily basis . . . and both we AND our brand loyalists loved every minute of it! With this type of culture, everyone and everything you do must match the positioning to stay true to your brand, and must be authentic to your tribe of consumers—your community. Fortunately, Oakley was always finding ways to drive the market forward with breakaway technologies, construction, or styling, not taking the time to consider what our competitors might be doing. This bred an attitude that matched our culture. Without being a leader in your category—one with premium positioning, best-in-class product, and a commitment from the top down—it is nearly impossible to authentically have the type of culture such as what we had at Oakley. This is a classic case of culture driving the brand, finding a persona that defined who we were and how we wanted to be perceived to the outside world, which bled into our internal bloodlines.

Now, it's time to ask yourself the hard questions:

Can you honestly say that those both inside and outside your brand understand your culture? More than understanding it, do you *embrace* it?

Brands that have what it takes to be visionary embrace the challenge of honestly examining their own culture and practices; those that have ostrich syndrome or a lack of commitment refuse to acknowledge their weaknesses, and as a result, the brand continues to rot from the head down.

I have been a part of visionary brands where this passion for its products, people, and processes flows throughout the entire organization. It is a beautiful thing to see a culture where principles are anchored into the foundational core of the brand and consistently ingrained into those working with and for the organization.

You can choose to embrace an authentic, no-BS, values-centered culture, or you can ignore the obvious and continue patching up the symptoms of a dying culture: turnover, declining profits/market share, evaporating passion, non-existent innovation, or copycat syndrome. The choice is yours as a brand leader. With no cultural commitment from the top—no vertically ingrained, values-centered, principles-managed culture built and implemented through your culture matrix—the base will either revolt or move on.

Those brands that anchor themselves in principles use their time to drive the brand forward, building passion within the organization and finding ways to beat their competition. The brands that choose not to define or adopt core principles are continually battling with internal dissatisfaction that comes with trying to understand what the brand stands for and where they are headed.

Staying true to who you are requires first understanding who you are, then building core cultural values that define what you are committed to as a brand. Your culture requires nourishment to grow and flourish, and it is up to you to ensure it is continually evangelized and embraced by all. When you let your guard down—not staying true to the foundational values-driven leadership culture you have passionately committed yourself to—the brand dies from the inside out.

"Culture is simply a shared way of doing something with a passion."

– Brian Chesky

THE PRODUCT VISION

"There's a way to do it better . . . find it."
— *Thomas Edison*

The **product ideation and execution process** of a brand is one the most complex, dynamic areas on the path to achieving visionary status. This is absolutely the one element of a successful formula that, if done correctly for a sustainable period of time and maintained within the brand, will set you apart for decades.

What sets great visionary brands apart from one another? A product ideation and lifecycle strategy that is second to none—one that is embraced by all of those associated with creating, driving, and protecting the brand's premium positioning.

Many product strategies change over the years, with shifts in how products are commercialized, purchased, delivered, and consumed. In each instance there are progressive updates, or new creation takes place. As a result, the way of doing things changes, commercialization timelines are reduced, processing speeds are increased, and our way of life is never the same. This presents a challenge to the brand itself, but not to the principles on which the company was founded at the outset.

With the pace of innovation, losing sight of your vision in order to see what is behind does not help you stay on course for what is ahead. Keep thinking differently. You have to set a creative path for the brand to drive towards, ensuring you do not go off course. In most companies, this future-oriented thinking that cuts through the fog is not proactively embraced, as it requires taking risks. All great products are driven by risk and realized by those who had the foresight to create and to travel where others dare not tread. Here's to the visionaries, the square pegs fitting into a round world. Visionary brands understand that what is ahead is more important than that which has been left behind. You may not know what is ahead, but you must always maintain your direction throughout this journey. The road less traveled, or ideally never traveled at all, is the one with the greatest adventure and reward. Move on and move ahead!

By taking this path, visionary brands embrace the sense of adventure, risk, and failure, but also know this journey is what eventually allows for the realization of truly once-in-a-lifetime, generational products. In reaching their destination, they have set themselves further apart from any potential competitors, setting the standard for their category and never relinquishing this lead. This is the ethos for all visionary brands.

So what are some of the common characteristics of visionary brands? How they are able to sustain and maintain a consistent flow of products while staying to their foundational positioning? Essentially, product vision breaks down into six truisms that you need to take to heart for the sake of your brand:

1. **Innovate, don't imitate**
2. **Create breakaway products**
3. **Build a drawdown product pipeline**
4. **Lead through extinction**
5. **The brand is the product**
6. **Take risks, break things**

Let's look at each of these guidelines a little more closely to see how to make sure your brand has a clear and effective product vision.

INNOVATE, DON'T IMITATE

Being able to create groundbreaking products comes through innovation and adaption, not imitation.

Now, I know Picasso had an enduring principle: "Good artists copy, great artists steal." There are times when this definitely works in the business world, but that is the exception, not the rule. Being able to develop a new revolutionary product through commercializing great ideas, innovations, or adapted technologies is a unique and invigorating process. These ideas adapted from other industries to satisfy needs in your market are game changers.

A great example of adaptable product ideation is Nike's "Flywire" technology. The product construction did not come from a competitive product, but rather from a structure not related to their industry: suspension bridges. The product team came across this inspiration while striving to answer a singular question in their work:

How can we create a minimalist shoe that has superior construction performance?

Rather than starting by building a new product from the ground up, the Nike product team turned to NASA for inspiration. They found Vectran, a fiber five times stronger than steel, flexible, and thinner than a human hair. Once they located the foundational product that they could adapt to realize their idea, the Flywire design was commercialized, and the footwear industry was changed forever through drawdowns, updates, and sport-specific models. All of this innovation was realized through product adaptation.

Determining, developing, and nurturing a culture of innovation is a key attribute to realizing your vision. Those who are followers will always be followers, but those who choose to lead the pack are innovators and clear the path for others to follow. So how do you create a culture of innovation?

- First, provide a clear anchoring strategy around what defines your brand and how you want to be perceived. Value is created through perception (good, better, best, premium versus commodity).
- Commit to failure. Take risks and blow things up. Find a better way—that is the only road to travel in order to disrupt your category. Define your strategy wrapped around building a sustainable pipeline of innovation.
- Define how the brand is interpreted to the outside world and how products will be marketed. Stay consistent, stay authentic.
- Determine how your pipeline of products will flow through your supply and demand cycle and respective distribution channels.
- Always provide category leadership. Be the voice others listen to and follow.

Visionary brands have these in common: what they create must be unique and not imitated. In other words, it must be innovative.

"Innovation" is a word tossed around very loosely by those who do not fully understand what it takes to be creative, but to those who are truly innovative, it has a much deeper meaning. Visionary brands actually live up to the meaning of the word, finding a better way or a more simplistic process and building it into the culture of their brand. Realizing a tangible product that matches this positioning is a powerful strategy for truly visionary brands.

There are many brands that rather publicly went through a maturation process when it came to implementing true innovation in their products. The most famous such case is Apple and Steve Jobs. By the time Steve returned to the company, the Apple brand had not only lost its way from a product standpoint, but also lost its passion and cultural direction. Steve redirected Apple, reinvigorated its passion, set a new course, and brought the brand back from extinction . . . but even more importantly, he brought the cultural foundation back into the bloodlines of Apple. Most brands that lose their way are not lucky enough to bring back their original visionary, one who personifies the brand and is able to convey what the future looks like and how they will adapt and succeed in this new world.

Apple is an example of a visionary brand that is driven by insanely great products—products that are truly innovative, not imitating their competitors. The best you can do if you're focused on imitating your competition is to make a better mousetrap, which risks losing both your first-mover advantage and abandoning the product pipeline of innovation. When you introduce a product into the pipeline that does not follow the same ideation process as previous products, the chain gets broken and needs to be rebuilt.

Visionary brands are built on this foundation of originality and authentication. Authentication is a blending of product and culture with an eye toward what is both right for the brand and needed by your community of advocates, whether they understand they need it or not. This is another trait seen in visionary brands: the ability to create a product concept and define its niche before anyone can see it with their eyes. "Believing is seeing" is what drives visionaries, not "seeing is believing." The former is innovative, creating what others cannot yet see; the latter is imitative.

Just as imitation can interrupt the product vision process, brands will often bring in those who have no passion for the brand, its products, or culture. I am not saying you cannot bring in smart outsiders, but be sure they understand the brand foundation, the culture they are entering, and what they will need to thrive and be successful. If you are not diligent in this process, you risk losing authenticity and product authentication. I have seen firsthand how brands lose their soul when this happens too frequently.

Being a visionary requires a top-down commitment to a strategic ideation process, clear product creation principles, and unwavering marketplace positioning in order to sustain brand equity. These must not be sacrificed for short-term gain. The world is too small to believe there will not be either authenticity lost or an evaporation of trust as a result of such a decision to sacrifice what you have built for the sake of immediate revenue gain.

As we have discussed, imitation is a short path to destruction while innovation provides a long-term road map to a clear product vision and a successful product pipeline. This is a pipeline that, if executed properly, will allow you to surf the open water and enjoy the freedom to innovate as a direct result of your leadership.

Remember, a key concept to realizing this innovation pipeline is through commercializing breakaway products—those ideas thought to be impractical or not needed, realized through brands that looked at the future differently. Let's take a closer look at this breakaway strategy . . .

CREATE BREAKAWAY PRODUCTS

Product creation is a unique process by which you must be able to not only think outside the box, but rather blow up the box and find a new way. What you're looking for is a new way to provide a product that simplifies, engages, enhances, or simply provides relief to our everyday life. Most are not previously known, are not progressive updates, but rather those products that set the standard for others to follow—the breakaway product.

In developing a breakaway product platform, there must be a method to the madness or all you will generate are great ideas with no ability to commercialize. The creative engine and the power triad are your internal support structures to building this platform with the product team being the key to bringing ideas to reality, creating truly authentic, **breakaway ideas**. By design, "breakaway" means your brand is disruptive by design, separating itself from the competition and providing ongoing category leadership. Some people may also reference "first mover" or "category creator" as industry terms that relate to breakaway products. This is accurate, but these are byproducts of a breakaway pipeline that consistently thinks differently and creates that what has not yet been developed. Recognize that your core audience is waiting for the next wave of unique, truly innovative products to hit the shores. Let them surf your pipeline!

If you have your sights set on building a visionary brand, being recognized as the consistent leader in your category, you must:

1. Give the product team the power to dream and fail. Reward excellent failure, as these are the stepping-stones to eventual success. Success without failure and disappointment is impossible.

2. Commit to category leadership from the top, and stay firm to your commitment. It will be difficult at times not to want to turn around and take the safe road; just don't do it!

3. Build a sustainable ideation process to build and effectively test your concepts. This will ensure not only that the product performance is best in class, but that the UX exceeds expectations.

4. Stay true to your brand foundation. Taking shortcuts or circumventing the process will only short-circuit

the business. Disrupt with product, execute the process.

5. Dream big, break things. Don't accept the world for the way it is currently, but rather for what you see it can be. Create the future!

This is a long process to achieving sustained breakaway product and process success, but once you have positioned yourself as the category leader, you are able to determine your desired price point, command the attention of brand advocates, and migrate your product down the demand curve through drawdowns.

The breakaway process is invigorating for the product team as it allows for a free flow of the ideation, providing broad boundaries to define the brand's future. These defined boundaries are needed in order to ensure ideas are not just good in theory, but can eventually be realized and commercialized in the marketplace. Lacking these boundaries and timelines there is little accomplished, and frustration is the end result.

A great example is car brands; specifically, the designers behind these companies. Having managed product and marketing for global brands, there can be no more frustrating experience for a designer than to continually see your beautiful concepts on paper being diluted through the commercialization process. Eventually, this mutation can take on the form of something unrecognizable from your original design. Can you imagine being in a role where every thought you provide, every suggestion you recommend is muted or diluted in some manner, taking on a completely different context than you intended? This is the life of car designers, whom I respect greatly—their imagination shows no bounds, and if cut loose it could reinvigorate an otherwise very stale industry. The context of this reference is boundaries, which can either stifle innovation or promote it. You must find a balance, and those who successfully found this balance are the visionaries with some of the world's greatest products. Set boundaries for practical commercialization; just do not stifle great ideas in the process.

Having a commercialization process for these products is one thing, but understanding market expectations and consumer needs is another. I have personally seen brands implode because they had no specific process to anticipate or evaluate market needs, as a result providing products nobody asked or wanted. This can be deadly for your brand, and if not corrected will be your demise. Your brand will only have sustained success if everyone participates as a team, adds value towards its commercialization, and promotes it once it is created.

Building a sustained flow of innovative, market-driving ideas is as much about the culture of the brand as it is about the products themselves. The culture defines your products, processes, and people. Without dedication to the foundational principles that define who you are, the process breaks apart and those visionary thinkers and future creators will not gravitate to your brand. Those who are at the top must shout to everyone inside the four walls of your machine, "We are committed to maintaining our leadership position as an authentic, market-driving visionary brand at all costs!" Be authentic, be committed, be real, be passionate, be creative.

Unless you are consistently and continually creating breakaway products (whether immediately commercialized for your market or put into the product pipeline) or disrupting your categories, you do not have an innovative culture. You're either making a better mousetrap or a drawdown to previous creations, neither of which defines a visionary brand. There is nothing inherently wrong with these options, but there will be an internal disconnect when the culture does not match positioning expectations. This creates confusion within the brand and a disconnect with those outside the brand.

It takes commitment to assure the foundation of innovation stays intact while maintaining the balance of what is right for the brand. This is why there are so few truly revolutionary leaders, ones who are calm when the outside voices get loud. Case in point: when there is a market disruption such as the financial meltdown or the COVID epidemic, you will be thrust into a crisis situation where short-term thinking and long-term strategy are at odds with one another. Staying true to the brand is much more difficult than it seems under these circumstances, and those who think logically, define potential outcomes, assess alternatives, and make clear decisions are the ones who come out the other side.

This ongoing and committed culture of producing breakaway products is achieved when you consistently and authentically execute your product ideation, testing, and commercialization process over a long period with a defined set of expectations for the brand. As a result, you build a loyal following and avoid any breakdowns in trust. True visionaries think beyond product—they ensure there is a clear path to innovation, rewarding both successes and failures throughout the commercialization process.

There are many parts to building a solid visionary foundation (see the Introduction), but assuring all brand pillars are created, communicated, and maintained is key to sustaining internal culture and revenue growth. Equity is built through a branding process, and is rooted in selling a desired lifestyle and providing premium products. However, in order to achieve this positioning, you must be thought of as a leader within your respective category, earning this right through consistent wins and products that have successfully sold at retail. Creating products that drive revenue, satisfy an unmet need, and establish a new category is an ongoing formula for success.

To recap, building a breakaway product culture must begin with a commitment from the top and end with a process that drives a sustained flow of innovative ideas that turn your vision into reality. By determining or satisfying a need, providing a product to meet this need, you are creating a flow of ideas that feed upon one another. Through this process, you now have a story to tell, one unique to your product that no one else can replicate. Be innovative, don't imitate. It is much harder to innovate, but this is the road you must take in order to attain premium status.

Having personally commercialized several patented (utility) breakaway products over the years, I can say you will find these are significantly easier to sell, and thus easier to provide the marketing team the juice needed to drive the brand engine. These are also the products that allow you to sustain your pipeline of innovation and long-term brand growth, eventually achieving broad market share across differing price point tiers and product categories.

BUILD A DRAWDOWN PRODUCT PIPELINE

With a solid innovation platform in place and a breakaway development mindset, the next strategic initiative a visionary brand undertakes for clarifying their product vision is creating a **drawdown pipeline** of products that squeezes the competition. A drawdown strategy is one that positions a premium across all price tiers within a product category. As I referenced earlier, a great example of this strategy being deployed is TaylorMade Golf.

When TaylorMade had a commanding market share within the golf club category, there were several price tiers they did not yet dominate. They were the clear leader at the premium price point level, but did not have a pipeline to satisfy the "good" and "better" levels. At the time they had a breakaway technology in the form of MWT (Moveable

Weight Technology), and had incorporated this into their top-tier products. In order to satisfy a mid-tier price point they created a sub-brand, removing the MWT flagship technology, and were thus able to build market share at the mid-tier price point without degrading brand equity. This was their first drawdown technology product.

But there was another tier to dominate: the "good." In order to create value without alienating both consumers and retailers, TaylorMade would move previous generations of products from "in-line" to good price point levels. This was a second drawdown strategy, completed with a previous generation of product and consequently not requiring further product development.

The last piece of the puzzle was to compress new technology innovations by 66% so new product generations would hit the shelf more frequently, giving the early adopters a reason to upgrade to the latest innovations. This also allowed the late majority an opportunity to upgrade to previous generations of this breakaway product.

In deploying this drawdown strategy at retail, TaylorMade was able to gain more than 18% market share with their core products across all channels of distribution. All without any degradation of brand equity or loyalty; in fact, both actually were enhanced by getting the product in the hands of their community sooner!

This is a key strategy, and I have seen competitors squashed by this being executed in the marketplace. The reason for its strategic effectiveness is it can be deployed by premium brands without having to apologize for any contradiction to their elite positioning. This strategy can be aggressive or passive, but those who have used it most successfully are ones aggressively implementing it across their distribution channels. In order to successfully deploy a drawdown program, you MUST have two pieces of this puzzle in place:

1. Relentless innovation ("innovate, don't imitate")
2. A breakaway product pipeline

To learn a little more about how the drawdown pipeline works, we can examine the **cycle of product life**. Few have mastered it, but most if not all visionary brands use this life cycle flow in order to drive long-term revenue without degrading brand equity.

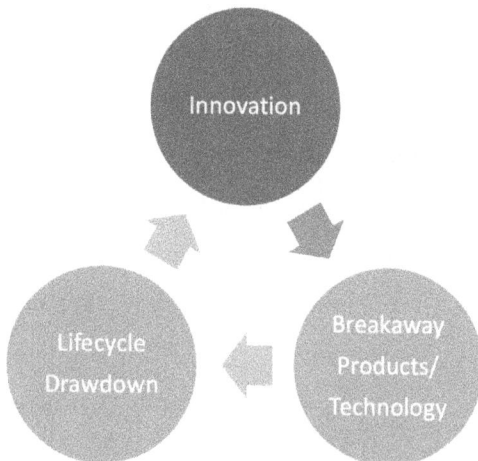

Product Lifecycle

The art of the drawdown strategy is to create a pipeline of breakaway products or technology through **hero products** (ones that are generations ahead of their time), then breaking those products down into adaptable pieces or migrating these pieces to lower price point options. These tiered products will move along the classic adoption curve relative to the aggressiveness of product line integration plan led by the power triad (product/marketing/sales teams). This can be either aggressive or very aggressive, relative to what you have coming through your pipeline. If you have a substantial backlog of breakaway innovations and the ability to adapt or migrate to new products, then you should be aggressive; if you are building this pipeline, then you should plan to be more passive.

Brands will base their marketing on this new technology until it is replaced by the next generation. The intention is to market your leadership position, then quietly move previous generations into lower price tiers and expanded distribution channels. By implementing this breakaway hero strategy, you are able to keep your premium positioning (price point/ margins) while maintaining brand equity and consumer goodwill. This also allows a brand to compress the adoption curve by releasing progressively newer or next-generation products in order to increase demand and limit supply.

An example of this breakaway (early adopters) and drawdown (late majority) strategy can be seen in the following chart. As you can see, an "innovators" breakaway curve is much steeper than a traditional adoption curve.

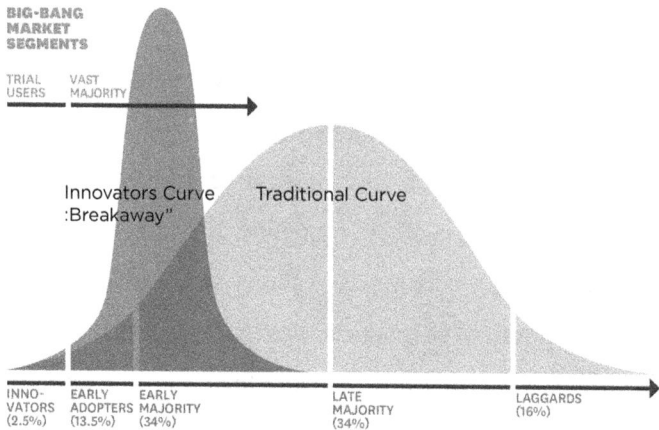

BIG-BANG
MARKET
SEGMENTS

TRIAL   VAST
USERS   MAJORITY

Innovators Curve   Traditional Curve
:Breakaway"

INNO-   EARLY   EARLY   LATE   LAGGARDS
VATORS   ADOPTERS   MAJORITY   MAJORITY   (16%)
(2.5%)   (13.5%)   (34%)   (34%)

The most recognizable visionary brand that has built, integrated, and grown relative to this strategy is of course Apple. Apple has a significant pipeline of products and technology and will continue to deploy these products across its channels of distribution. It has a definitive strategy of migrating product across the traditional curve while promoting the next generation. People do not necessarily need to upgrade to the new iPhone, but it is the constant marketing push that pulls them online or in-store to get that new feature not available on their current generation. This is the start of the innovators curve, and ends with previous generations moving along the traditional curve.

In addition to creating new products, Apple also is relentless in building their eco-system—the "stickiness" of the brand as a whole. This was a strategy originated by Steve Jobs, and has allowed the company to go from the brink of bankruptcy to becoming the world's most iconic, valuable brand. Now, I am not saying drawdowns were the only reason for this reversal, but it certainly played a large part in its turnaround and long-term success. This two-tier adoption strategy is what continues to drive these premium brands to significant long-term growth. The irony with this strategy is almost all the brand or product awareness marketing spending is for new products, while the majority of the revenue is driven by previous generation products.

With this product strategy firmly integrated into your brand ethos, you can now focus on what is next for the brand and your community. Being able to price at a premium level with a continual flow of revolutionary products, while also utilizing drawdown technologies through previous generations of products, has effectively squeezed the lifeblood out of many competitors.

The drawdown mentality is a very disciplined approach to not killing the golden goose that got you where you are today. Visionary brands have effectively deployed the drawdown strategy through the creation of breakaway ideas brought to life and embraced by their generation of consumers. I say *their* generation as most tech is adopted by a younger generation first before moving to other demographics. Understanding this is key to building a successful long-term visionary brand, as generational adoption is integral to ensuring sustainable growth. The broader the appeal, the harder it is to position yourselves as unique and develop elite positioning. This is certainly not the case with all brands, but the general principle does make long-term growth much easier to forecast.

In contrast to innovators like Apple, I have personally seen imitator companies go on to become successful, but only when they ride the coattails of visionary brands. These imitators are like leeches that attach themselves to successful brands, knocking off products that have gained traction in the marketplace. They introduce products on the back end of the adoption curve (late majority) and are not considered industry/category leaders, their only discernable POD being price point. These are herd companies that relentlessly churn out lower-priced variations of products released by authentically innovative brands. Contrast this strategy with those visionary brands that consistently build and grow their pipeline of innovation, allowing them to create ongoing value for their customers through the product drawdown strategy.

As we have discussed, being an imitator is not a strategy for invigorating a brand. Following the success of other companies is only a plan to ring the cash register, which for some is the overriding goal. I mention this strategy as a measure of what some companies settle for versus a strategy to maintain category leadership.

The most effective way to fight this type of competition is to ensure your brand thrives, and you engage with those who love what you create and the lifestyle you represent. No company can copy these qualities; lifestyle trumps all. Stick to what brought you to this point—a clear, cohesive plan for defining your product strategy, and continuing to be a relentless innovator—and leave the imitation to others. Make sure you continue to communicate this commitment through the bloodlines of the entire brand. They need to hear this brand strategy evangelized every day, and do not waver or be influenced by others looking to eliminate or dilute what you have achieved.

LEAD THROUGH EXTINCTION

Once a visionary brand has successfully executed a breakaway/drawdown strategy, they must then build a bridge to ensure the product lifecycle does not become overextended. In order to sustain a consistent flow of products from your pipeline, you must bring some products to **extinction**, sometimes at the height of their popularity. It is critical, but also very risky to implement this strategy, as you are betting the company on the next generation of products. However, **unless you risk something, you gain nothing.**

As discussed earlier, one of the most recognizable case studies of product lifecycle saturation was the Sony Walkman. This was a breakaway product when first introduced, but Sony did not fully embrace the drawdown and extinction mentality, instead deciding to let it ride for some thirty years with only minor revisions along the way. This strategy proved to be successful for a time, but this is a rare case. The danger with deploying such a strategy is you can get ambushed by your competitors, and you inevitably become a follower, no longer a leader. Having the market perception of being an innovative leader in your category carries with it prestige and privilege.

Most companies would assume any brand that has deployed the breakaway strategy must have a new product in the pipeline that will change the norm, establish a new way of thinking, or redefine a process. This was not the case with Sony and the Walkman—revolutionary in its day, had a nice run for some 20 years, but eventually died a slow death in its last 10. The clincher was when Apple introduced the iPod, at which point it was game over for the Walkman. Ironically, the Walkman was an inspiration to Steve when coming up with a better way to listen to music that was not so cumbersome or limited in portability. In analyzing the Walkman lifecycle, Apple knew better than to repeat the mistakes of Sony, incorporating extinction in their product pipeline and having the courage to pull products at the peak of their popularity to keep their community hungry for what's coming next.

I reference this case in order to better establish that truly visionary brands will always push products through the lifecycle pipeline, then move on to the next innovation, sometimes even when people may not agree with the timing. This type of brand ethos is very challenging for those on the front lines driving the ideation process, but it is also the most invigorating part of their leadership role.

Having led design teams with some of the most iconic brands in the world, I've seen visionary brands driven by the next great idea, not by the one that has already been born or one someone else has already commercialized. A constant drive to innovate is what fuels the creative engines of these design teams, and why it is so critical for brands to integrate a product extinction life cycle before they arrive at the saturation point. The peak of demand is when most visionary brands are looking to bring new products to the market. This creates a compressed supply and demand curve, a quick-to-market execution, and a drawdown opportunity with the new crown jewel most if not all of their early adopters have been waiting for since the last version was launched.

An interesting facet of product extinction is the fact that the lifecycle has contracted drastically as demand for the next generation has increased. This is directly correlated to the need for a pipeline of product innovations that can be commercialized in succession, effectively squeezing your competitors. Having an ingrained culture built around this extinction mentality allows the brand to sustain a clean, sustainable product lifecycle flow. Great ideas can only be commercialized if the old ones move on.

"If we don't cannibalize ourselves, someone else will."

– Steve Jobs

Cannibalization in the marketplace is another term for making a better way or a better product, not recreating or disrupting the market or category itself. Being able to move on from a product before it hits the stage where it is being cannibalized by competitors is critical to the success of a visionary brand. Knowing when to remove a product from the market is as hard if not harder than releasing the product to the market, but is a critical strength of a visionary brand.

Building a consistent and sustainable product extinction lifecycle flow creates limited supply, increasing demand on both the back end (drawdown) and the front end (breakaway). This has driven many brands to become some of the most valuable on the planet, such as Apple, Microsoft, Nike, adidas, TaylorMade, and Microsoft. These are iconic brands that have stood the test of time by building an innovative pipeline of products or services supported by a breakaway culture. Each of these brands succeeds by creating and adapting over a series of product iterations, adopting technologies that drive customer demand and manipulate supply cycles through planned product extinction.

Building a product innovation pipeline that can sustain continual and more rapid product extinction is where successful visionary brands move beyond their competitors. By holding to this vision rooted in these principles, you too will successfully build sustainable brand value for both your shareholders and your customers.

THE BRAND IS THE PRODUCT

In defining your product vision, you must first understand who you are and what you stand for. If you do not know this, do not expect your customer or brand advocate to know. This is a foundational principle of visionary brands—all have clearly and cohesively defined their brand and can convey it in simple language understood by all.

This is critical not only for those driving the idea and design engine, but also for those running operations, finance, sales, and all areas of the brand, as they are some of your most important bloodlines. These are the ones who believe in what you stand for and know they are part of its creation and ongoing survival. Stick to your defined anchoring principles and your brand ethos and you will have a loyal following for your brand.

Product vision is driven by the defined positioning, culture, category, and voice of the brand. In other words, the vision is defined by the brand itself. You will hear designers ask of a new idea, "Is it right for the brand?" This is the right question to ask as part of your ideation process, but it is not where that process should end. If you detour around your anchored principles as a brand, you lose both trust and equity.

In executing the product vision, I have seen many brands simply look to create a better mousetrap as opposed to finding a better way (think of the Walkman's inspiration to Steve Jobs). By following the process of defining only what the market needs instead of what is best for your customer and the market, you set yourself up for failure. Short-circuiting the product innovation pipeline in favor of chasing market trends will only create distrust with your brand advocates. Visionary brands understand the market, are loyal to the brand's foundation, and are constantly in touch with their influencers.

The product vision is set and must be committed to at all levels, from the top down. Not just some of the time but *all* of the time! It is crucial the leaders define the brand (although all are involved in creating the culture), but more importantly, that they know what is driving the culture—inevitably, it needs to be the product vision and lifestyle. In short, your product vision *is* your brand, so you need to set it and maintain it carefully.

If you look at most iconic brands, each has an aspirational connotation built into the product itself. Building this aspirational culture requires having a clearly defined yet adaptable product vision for the brand. The culture created through product vision is a clear competitive advantage, as long as the brand's foundation is not compromised over time.

Again, I have seen many brands that once were aspirational and had a loyal following either completely crumble or slowly leak their brand equity over time. This type of brand equity damage is virtually impossible to recover from, and this is why taking a short-term approach can be so deadly. Brand equity is earned over time with continual, revolutionary products that match the foundational vision. Visionary brands are very careful to treat this privilege with great care. The most visual piece of a brand is its product, so do all that you do with great care and do what is right for the brand.

Visionary brands that have successfully navigated their product vision and anchored their principles also have a process in place to ensure a consistent flow of great ideas that match the brand positioning. This is how successful brands think when it comes to setting, creating, and building their product vision for the company. This ensures everyone overseeing this product process understands expectations and how to be great caretakers of the brand. It also ensures that anyone who comes on board understands your expectations as well. An important aspect to the livelihood of a brand, yet oftentimes overlooked.

So, how do you make sure your product vision supports the kind of brand you want to build? A solid product vision has many variables and components, both tangible and intangible. When brands look to establish this foundation, it must be cohesive and vertical in its composition, regardless of product category or channel segmentation. This means the brand must have a consistent, recognizable visual and cultural language. In the case of consumer brands this would consist of marketing strategy, visual imagery, verbal communications, logo, product construction, performance characteristics, specific channel use (running, outdoor, etc.), and merchandising presentations.

In the case of tech brands, this would consist of branding, UX, styling, feel, touch, and visual presentation. Each holds a unique piece to the overall product vision, but collectively is a recognizable product driven through the foundational vision. Those who have achieved their product vision through internal process and external marketplace execution have successfully created a visual/verbal positioning with their consumer. This is a significant point of difference between a brand and a commodity. You may be able to knock off a product, but you cannot recreate the lifestyle associated with being part of a brand foundation. These are the brands you recognize not just by their logo, but also by their design language, aesthetics, styling, colors, packaging, merchandising, advertising, and more. They have through vertical omni-focused design and positioning subtly built an image over time that has characterized them as best in class, a direct result of successfully executing and committing to their product vision.

Executing the product vision requires a talented product team that is able to achieve creative excellence while navigating potential brand landmines. Even inside visionary brands there will be a constant need to fight the temptation to cut corners or release product before it is ready for primetime. These are enemies of building an ongoing innovative pipeline and disruptive ideas that when accomplished further distance the brand from its competitors. Many times this type of culture can be frustrating for the creators, the dreamers who are not used to this type of product lifecycle creation process, one that may not always approve of what a designer considers a disruptive yet commercially viable product, especially with risk-averse individuals within the leadership of a brand. This goes back to why a brand needs strong visionary leadership at the top in order to secure and maintain the best industry talent. Building a brand through category leadership requires the most imaginative talent and the freedom to create and support to fail.

Truly visionary brands will have an evangelist at the top, ready to take the lead and move products along the lifecycle plan. Sometimes they may be wrong, but more often than not, they are dead-on with what the brand should be doing next in order to create a continual cycle of market-driving products.

The product is the brand. Be sure it matches the vision!

TAKE RISKS

"A person who never made a mistake never tried anything new."
— Albert Einstein

Risk is part of the visionary brand's DNA. This foundational characteristic is found in most brands considered the category leader . . . and is the single most important quality most competitors avoid while trying to stay relevant in their market. They do not want to risk failure, so they leave it to the experts—those brands that have a culture, team, and history of leading the way forward. Without these revolutionary brands, they would have nothing to produce and no revenue to speak of. *You* must be the one to move the bar, not the competition. This disruptive mindset and strategy invigorates a product team and sets the path for long-term creative genius to thrive. It must be accepted and embraced that successful failures are part of the process and are necessary in order to ensure all options are exhausted.

Successful visionary brands do not "tolerate" failure, but rather embrace it. If you are not failing, then you are not attempting to find solutions. Solutions without failure are impossible, so why not embrace this strategy?

Fail often, fail fast, and move on . . .

Unfortunately, all too many leaders are not comfortable with risking failure. This ingrained mindset contributes to frustration, lowering the bar and increasing employee turnover by killing company morale. Those at the top are solely responsible for solidifying or completely changing this culture: risk-averse leadership will attract only those with the same play-it-safe mindset. Creating a culture of product or category disruption is risky, but seeing the end result of this commitment gives a brand the fuel to drive their category leadership.

Failures should be learned from, not punished, in order to execute a successful product vision. Visionary brands have a leader who is committed to both driving this strategy and ensuring the profitability of the company at the same time. This can be a daunting task, but when consistently, authentically implemented and anchored inside the company, it is a strategy for long-term market share growth. This is why you will see a passionate leader at the forefront of product introductions; they are side by side with the teams throughout the entire process and are entrenched on a daily basis until it is unveiled to the world.

With this process, there is a balancing act that needs to happen—a happy medium among disruption, commercial viability, and your brand's foundational principles. This balancing act is why true, authentic leadership needs to take the reins. If there is not a singular vision ensuring each product is right for the brand, is market-driving, and is commercially viable, you will end up with a company that has no direction or viability. This is where a great leader is crucial—a brand needs someone who has a command of what is being brought to market as well as when, how, and where this is accomplished. Most if not all visionary brands have such a person to drive their future.

Remember, being a leader does not make you a visionary; this is truly a rare trait. The visionary in this context is one who creates, protects, evangelizes, and promotes the brand's product vision. Too many times a leader thinks they are visionary, and this can have devastating efforts on the development of the company. Allowing for a complete disconnect between what you are good at versus what you are not capable of doing effectively is deadly for a brand.

Unfortunately, too many leaders do not have this awareness, and even worse, there is no one inside the company willing to risk telling them! Cultivate the personal awareness to know your strengths along with your weaknesses, as this is critical to gaining the respect of your team and the company as a whole. They have entrusted you with the keys to the brand; just make sure you know how to drive it.

And when you are behind that wheel, you can choose to drive the brand where you think best, and go fast or slow . . . just do not stay in park, paralyzed in the face of making a decision. For better or worse, making no decision is the worst-case scenario. If you do not know how to drive the brand product vision, ensure you have a good partner while you focus on fine-tuning the engine!

"Safe is risky."

– Seth Godin

Now that we have set the expectation of the brand foundation from the top down, it's time to understand how visionary brands disrupt through taking risks. The following principles, driven by championing risk, are ingrained into all visionary brands and flow through their bloodlines every second. This embracing of risk allows them to thrive in a chaotic world.

Product Vision to Reality Ethos

- Don't play it safe.
- Make mistakes, don't try to avoid them.
- Experiment.
- Take initiative, don't wait for instructions.
- Break things, welcome destruction.
- Focus on opportunities, not problems.
- Never give up or compromise on a great idea that will further our cause.
- There's no guarantee of success; a sure thing is probably not innovative.
- Don't bloody the water.
- Reinvent yourself before the competition.
- Always think outside the box!

Visionary brands are ones that disrupt the status quo and create proactively (as opposed to reactively), ensuring the world is constantly changing to the betterment of everyone. Of course, not all change is good—you must measure each change you are thinking about making against your brand's foundation to ensure you are genuinely creating for the sake of improvement, not for short-term greed. Being true to your vision and your foundation always enhances long-term value for your customer and brand equity for the company.

Disruption is the end result of taking risks. Visionary brands understand the correlation between the two and know you cannot have one without the other. So if you do not take risks and do not embrace failure, the end result will *not* be a breakaway, disruptive product, but rather a breakdown of the innovation pipeline. However, if you embrace risk-taking, celebrate failure, and have a commitment to both from the top down, then inevitably disruption is your reward.

In my direct experience with and analysis of visionary brands, I have found this risk factor to be a common thread to their eventual success. Those who change the world—who "put a dent in the universe," as Steve Jobs said—are those leaders in their channel or category who continue to thrive in good times and bad. These brands are the disruptors; most are household names, and most are aspirational both in the lifestyle and products they create. With this aspirational positioning comes the privilege of top-tier price points, along with a command of the market segment development. Traditionally these visionary, disruptive brands are the ones that pull in early adopters at all levels, eagerly awaiting the next product evolution (or revolution) from their brand. I say "their brand" in the context of a feeling of being part of something bigger than just a product—a lifestyle that is embraced.

By embracing risk, many of these brands have found a way to manipulate the market commercialization rates and expedite the adoption curve. This is executed by brands that have built a value chain of products with a consistent flow of breakaway products with drawdown technologies. Taking risks and creating a disruptive product mentality gives the product team a foundation from which to realize ideas to move the brand forward and leave competitors in the rearview mirror. This hard-charging, take-no-prisoners approach is good for the longevity of the brand, ensuring you do what is right for the brand, not what the market wants. If Henry Ford had asked the consumer what they wanted, we would still be riding horses. You must find the future and provide what others cannot see or what they say is impractical. Again, this comes with caveats, but when you position your brand correctly and have a product vision to match, the market will see you as the leader and expect you and your brand to take charge.

The ability to anticipate what your consumers need in order to improve their lifestyle before they realize it is a unique trait reserved for proactive, risk-taking visionaries. This means proactively knowing what is next, putting resources toward its creation, and being willing to work through difficulties and failures. Playing it safe may be a foundational principle of commodity brands, but it is a character flaw in visionary brands. Do you aspire to be a visionary or a commodity?

There is no guarantee of success when you take risks; however, history has proven that it is those who take risks who are the ones most likely to achieve success. Establishing and committing to a culture of innovation and failure through risk creates a bond that solidifies the greatest product teams on the planet. These teams, entrusted with the future evolution of the brand, understand and embrace this concept to survive.

Hang on and enjoy the ride, stay true to who you are, embrace risk, and create the future!

THE ECOSYSTEM

Visionary brands find a way to create an **ecosystem** of products, ones that stick with a consumer wherever they communicate, visit, work, exercise, dine, drive or travel. Whether at home or traveling, being able to access the ecosystem when and where needed is now second nature to most consumers. A successful product ecosystem is an extremely user-friendly but sophisticated level of products, each of which independently serves a purpose, but collectively are indispensable components of the larger system. An ecosystem creates multiple fully-integrated consumer touchpoints, allowing your brand to build a relationship with your customer, as opposed to creating independent islands of engagement, none of which establish an ongoing relationship.

This was not always the go-to strategy for brands, as most did not have the foresight or the technology to execute such a plan. But with the progression of new and emerging technologies, social media, software as a service (SaaS), and other integration platforms, this strategy is now tangible. The evolution of the internet in combination with the revolution in product development has created the ability for brands to build an ecosystem for their hard-wired products, interactive digital components, and social engagement. When brought together, these ecosystems have become indispensable to our daily lives, to the point where their absence leaves a vacuum. Can you imagine now not having a smartphone? Or not having cloud access, or streaming capabilities? What used to be a luxury is now commonplace.

In defining their digital ecosystems, visionary brands took into account not only the product itself, but the user experience (UX) as well. Being able to create a sophisticated product while making it simple to understand is a beautiful thing only true artists can realize. But the ecosystem is a critical piece of the overall visionary brand's puzzle—without it, they sit on an island, isolated from reality.

Of course, integration by itself does not make for a successful ecosystem; it is the UX that allows your adoption rate to skyrocket. As I have observed throughout my years with global brands, many have succeeded at building a loyal community of followers, but few have succeeded in bringing them fully into their ecosystem. You must have a plan, one that is seamless and cohesive. The brand with best-in-class product draws the consumer in, but it is the ecosystem that keeps them in your world.

Because so many pieces are involved in creating an ecosystem, it can be easy to lose sight of your overriding objective. Keeping things on track is the role of tech integrators; the ecosystem interface and engagement strategy should be led by those artists who understand the overall experience and how it should flow (see "The Artist" below). To return to the musical analogy from earlier in the book: your team of tech experts, artists, and creators should have guidance about how the instruments will integrate within the orchestra—in other words, a conductor. Visionary brands have figured out that to effectively and efficiently deploy these components, the ecosystem must be rehearsed and properly arranged in order to know how the instruments sound together before playing to a crowd. When the music sounds beautiful and the instruments know their parts, you are ready to go live, and not a moment before.

Case in point: Apple started its revolution with just one product (the iPod), but had other structures in place to ensure this product did not stay static. Interconnectivity was key to building their ecosystem strategy—it was immediately paired with iTunes, getting the customers to invest in other interconnected products right out of the gate.

When you properly plan your ecosystem, you will have already mapped out your brand's destiny. No one knows what you will encounter on your journey, but at least you will have mapped a course to your planned destination. This first-mover advantage with a breakaway product can move you literally generations ahead of your competition, and the ecosystem will ensure you have control over the environment and experience each consumer has with your brand.

Every visionary brand since Apple has adopted some type of ecosystem strategy, and each has evolved in order to stay ahead of the technology curve. Staying static while others continue to invest in their culture, products, technology, and ecosystem is a recipe for disaster. Even worse, by not investing in their near-term and long-term future through an integrated brand ecosystem, brands risk losing touch with their consumers, each of whom has a choice in brands. Just make sure they always stay engaged and attached to your ecosystem.

Provide structure, provide ease of use, continually and relentlessly adapt, personally communicate, and provide value. These are all key points when planning your strategy for creating and implementing a brand ecosystem. It is not a matter of "if," but rather "how" and "when" you create your ecosystem. You are already behind by not having started, so start now!

Be proactive and be sure to map out your ecosystem strategy . . . but make sure you make it dynamic! The world moves fast, and you need to make sure you stay ahead of the movement. Ecosystem execution is a key ingredient to the recipe for success for visionary brands. Being able to draw customers into your community, engage with them, and personalize their experience will continue to help your brand evolve, providing more value to their day-to-day lifestyle.

THE FUEL

The **fuel** is what drives great brands to market aspirational products, create an authentic culture, and further solidify their premium positioning. The synergy realized through the power triad culminates in a successful product launch and acceptance by your core consumer. The fuel takes the form of best-in-class marketing across all levels of your brand communications and consumer engagements, both visually and verbally. Ignite it inside your brand and you will feel it across your entire organization and your community. It's the motivation, the enthusiasm for your brand's foundational principles that keeps your customers coming back and your team passionately driving your future.

Fuel, the marketing strategy that drives your brand, has become one of the most important components to successfully gaining market share and brand equity. While the continual progression of digital marketing engagement across advertising platforms (social, digital, sponsorships, etc.) has increased, the time window in which you can make an impact on your customer has been steadily decreasing. This provides a challenging backdrop to those brands looking to move out of the noise and into their own quiet space. Find a way to quickly connect through aspirational messaging with authentic products.

The thing about fuel is that it runs out if you don't top it off now and then. Your destiny is in your hands, so you must ensure it is carefully managed. This comes in the form of consistently reiterating your commitment to your ongoing foundational principles—*why* you exist. Visionary brands are constantly injecting this why into the brand in all areas, both inside and outside the company.

Jim Jannard, the visionary founder of Oakley, always made a point of "re-energizing" the team, never letting us forget what we stood for as a brand. He would give inspirational speeches that built a passion for the brand and pride in being a part of its ongoing success. By injecting this brand inspiration into Oakley through visual (posters, videos, sponsorships) and verbal communications every day, Jim provided a great working experience and fostered pride in what we achieved. Again, as with any messaging, this was reinforced with more than just words; there was also plenty of visual messaging throughout HQ that served as a continual reminder of the dedication of the brand and the founder himself.

Oakley HQ – The Bloodline
Disruptive by Design – The Injection

Oakley was a brand that embraced disruption, not just with product but in everything we did each day. Whether in product, processes, marketing, engagement, or just being different than the rest, we succeeded where others failed, and this fuel drove us to achieving global market share, a dominating product category share, and revenue in excess of $1 billion.

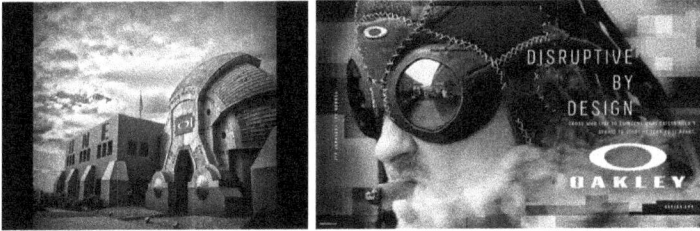

Having those visionary leaders who inspire the masses from the top down drives a passion for the brand and loyalty to its foundation. The fuel is supplied by the brand leader.

And just what does it look like to add that fuel to your brand? How does a visionary brand define, create, and successfully grow through its messaging and positioning? Regardless of the product, visionary brands are able to inject both **inspirational** and **aspirational** lifestyle messaging for its consumers, creating a very strong connection point in their daily lives. This connection point eventually turns into your community, and it's where your customers' loyalty to your brand starts. In our new dynamic, digital age this may be where the relationship starts, but can usually end there as well. If you break trust, confuse your messaging, or disconnect with your core, this is a slow leak that can quickly turn into a gaping hole, flushing all the great work out with it.

The idea of inspiring your consumers to achieve more through your products or technology is where visionary brands build a dedicated consumer following. In this age of digital destruction for brick-and-mortar retail, having the ability to create, engage with, and activate a base of followers (in other words, the ability to fuel your community) is integral to long-term success and viability. Inspire your customers to follow an aspirational lifestyle with your brand and no other company will be able to replicate it.

> "The most important thing is to try and inspire people so that they can be great in whatever they want to do."
>
> – *Kobe Bryant*

You will find that many diversified brands have aspiration as a cornerstone to their ongoing success: Nike, adidas, Ralph Lauren, and more. But you cannot be a premium brand unless you have defined your aspirational positioning and are able to consistently deliver this message and value proposition to your target consumer. Fortunately, this can come about organically through staying true to your foundational principles and living up to them authentically through your brand's culture—if you know who you are, there's no need to fake it.

In creating their inspirational marketing campaign "Just Do It," Nike was able to inspire the masses. The intent behind the campaign was to *inspire* individuals to achieve *aspirational* goals, with the product being the mechanism to assist them in achieving the goal. This was a brilliant campaign, as it was the first of its kind to drive messaging beyond product to a desired lifestyle. This would turn out to be a generational campaign— it was timeless, and not specific to a sport, gender, or race. "Just Do It" was a campaign to get people active, get them engaged and off the couch.

This is how you add the fuel to drive a brand—not through products, but through messaging to their loyal community, to let them know that the brand is here to help in achieving their goals. Brand, product, positioning and engagement—key pieces of the puzzle to achieving visionary marketing, and together they add to your brand's fuel.

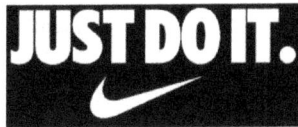

JUST DO IT.

All right, so it's clear why fueling your brand is necessary, and that it takes equal parts inspiration and aspiration. But just how is that achieved? What fuels a visionary brand?

INSPIRE THROUGH PERSONALIZATION

If you're driving a premium brand, you'll obviously need premium-grade fuel in the engine for ultra-performance. In order to maintain your strategy for maintaining and growing a premium brand, you can't just invest in product creation; you must also invest in the development of the messaging, marketing, and merchandising. To be perceived as premium, the message must match the reality at all levels of consumer engagement, from the anticipation to the purchase to the activation and eventual use. Each level of engagement is a point where visionary brands separate themselves from the competition, knowing each point of contact is critical to the overall success of the brand. And the best way to manage this engagement is through **personalization**.

Inspiring your community through personalization is the holy grail for visionary brands. Achieving this strategy successfully will give you access to massive amounts of data, metric analysis, and dynamic reporting in order to sharpen your focus. The most efficient way to gather this information and decipher what is needed versus what is not is by using AI (artificial intelligence); in order to provide accurate individualized data, targeted down to the consumer level, the amount of analysis that must be computed, regurgitated, and spit out into a legible format is mind-boggling.

But oh, the things you can do with that data once you have it! Personalization is a key strategy for demonstrating you understand the wants, needs, and desires of your community. This is your chance to move beyond talking about yourself, finding a way to talk about your customer through your community and providing a solution to their personal needs.

Here's the tricky part about showing you understand the values that drive your customers: you need to make sure you actually do understand them. Visionary brands are very sensitive to the obtrusive nature of communicating directly with their community, and are always ensuring they are providing continual value with every touchpoint, every communication. They are careful to identify points that are important to their community and drill down to the consumer level—sharing general information, personalized recommendations, convenience programs, or some other benefit to show the additional value provided by being part of the brand's community. This value is triggered in the mindset of your customer each time they engage with your brand; always provide ongoing value beyond product, and deliver consistent, value-driven messaging that keeps them engaged.

Measuring long-term consumer value through tangible metrics is key to predictability of both brand equity and revenue growth. This was a measure previously not attainable but is now a key digital dashboard to the ongoing heartbeat of any brand. Pre-purchase acquisition costs, transaction value, turn rate, and post-purchase value are also key metrics. In continually measuring the impact brand campaigns have on these metrics, a brand can more easily pivot in the direction where their investment will be maximized. These campaigns and investments can be built around demo profile, category opportunity, and lifestyle tiers. The more focused a brand is around refining these targeted campaigns, the better they are able to personalize the UX, as a result enhancing loyalty and defining lifetime value.

On that note, personalization offers visionary brands several opportunities to build loyalty in their community. This can be achieved by providing discounts, events, pre-releases, classes, product information, or some other value or convenience not offered by third-party sellers. The community you build should be treated with TLC, and personalization is a way for visionary brands to show appreciation for their loyalty.

Visionary brands recognize what it takes in order to execute this new method to communicating with their customer without being obtrusive and yet providing tangible value. Like most of the facets of a premium brand, this is difficult to achieve and even more difficult to sustain, but it must be executed flawlessly and consistently to maintain your leadership position.

BRAND AMBASSADORS

Clearly, keeping the fire of your brand fed with plenty of fuel isn't an easy task. It's fortunate that you don't have to do it all on your own! In order to support the internal team, visionary brands utilize **brand ambassadors**. These are the individuals who carry the brand's voice beyond the four walls of the company, the ones who are the most passionate users of the brand's products and are consistently promoting the product benefits.

The key is finding ambassadors who are authentic to their category. If you are a running brand, find an authentic runner; if you are a football brand, find an elite (NFL) player. It seems simple, but most companies do not understand the value this provides to a brand. Along with being authentic, make sure they have a following, one you can leverage.

For this strategy to work as planned, the brand ambassadors' reach in combination with their voice needs to be authentic, meaning they are always honest in their opinion. To be honest, though, authentic ambassadors can run both ways, for good or bad. Although most brands feel this honesty is too risky to engage with ambassadors, visionary brands feel it is imperative in order to get a broad user base to test its products. Risky or not, you must believe in your product in order to lead your category—give your ambassadors a voice and you will be rewarded by your community of followers. Importantly, their communication runs two ways: they can communicate your brand's messaging to your customer community, and they can communicate the community's thoughts and needs back to you. This is the role of your ambassadors; they are the external voice and the ones who promote your creations.

Brand ambassadors must be very carefully selected, as they are an extension of your brand, and are reflective of your product and your culture. They are the ones who will let you know about the acceptance or rejection of specific features and the overall impression of your brand's newest creation. For that reason, they must be authentic and honest with both you and the community at large, or they will lose trust among the rest of your customers, which undercuts why you are engaging with them in the first place.

Be selective, but also be proactively engaged with your brand ambassadors, as they will give you reach beyond what the normal digital metrics can provide. They give you a "ground force" of visual and verbal tangible touchpoints, providing a look into your customers' lives seldom achieved through digital dashboards. This is a dynamic, rich partnership, and one that should provide a mutually beneficial result. The ability to either challenge or confirm the product team's intuition through human touch is a powerful addition to the overall brand livelihood. Visionary brands are able to balance these two feedback channels and find a way to maximize the contribution of both, providing for an enhanced product or lifestyle brand experience.

When building the platform for communicating with your brand ambassadors, you must tier these ambassadors into channel-specific groups (running, biking, football, baseball, etc.), ensuring each is authentic, actively participating and believes in the foundational principles of the brand. This is needed in order to gain the trust of the product team and a deep understanding of the brand and its foundation. Otherwise, you will run into ulterior motives, or worse, inaccurate reviews that will be detrimental to the brand. With the digital world we live and breathe in, you must be checking on your "brand radar" every day, ensuring you are watching for those storms that can cause a disaster if you are not properly prepared.

Visionary brands engage with their ambassador community throughout the creation process, as they can provide feedback for the product team when necessary and guide the development of the latest product. This is why the vetting process is very important. It is better to have a few *great* ambassadors than a lot of *good* ambassadors. The latter are harder to engage with, while the former proactively embrace the brand and further its mission.

Bringing ambassadors into the creation process also increases their investment in the finished product. Once the product has been released, ambassadors will be fully aware of the amount of work that has gone into realizing this product vision, and thus are more passionate when it comes to promoting its authentic benefits. This builds mutual respect between the product team and those who support the vision and are committed to its brand strategy. Finally, once the product has been commercialized, translating your product vision to the outside world will be front and center for your brand ambassadors.

Making sure you have a translatable, easily understood vision requires the mastery of a visionary brand. Many brands have innovative products, yet find themselves in the position of being unable to properly translate the who, what, when, why, and where it is needed in our world, and specifically in each category. Having brand ambassadors who have been proactively involved throughout the creation process allows a brand to translate the vision, its tangible features, and its lifestyle benefits most effectively.

I cannot stress enough how important it is to take good care of your brand ambassadors. In the ever-changing landscape of consumer acquisition, it is critically important to coordinate, control, and manage your brand's messaging, both verbal and visual. Each of these is a subliminal touchpoint with your current and potential brand advocates. Any disconnect with lifestyle positioning and reality (products, promotion, channel) will result in a loss of trust, long-term consumer value, and predictable revenue growth.

It is clear that maintaining a customer who is already engaged with your brand is much easier and less costly than acquiring new customers. Always take care of who you have acquired first, enhancing their UX with your brand before engaging with those who are not yet part of your community. And by maintaining the enthusiasm of your team and your brand ambassadors, and by keeping your community at large inspired through personalization, you'll have a brand you won't need to worry about keeping fueled.

THE UX

A seamless user experience (UX) should always be the goal for any premium brand. The UX is a multifaceted puzzle built from the foundational principles of the brand itself, and as such you always need to be looking out for consumer time and value when it comes to UX. Being able to provide a seamless, fully integrated brand experience rather than a disjointed UX is a clearly defined point of difference over your competition. Think beyond the purchase cycle; visionary brands extend the UX into all areas of the company, and the way a brand interacts at these levels will by design create an unforgettable UX.

By example, think of when you engage with a brand. Whether product, information, events, or some other value-driven need, it is always the experience that sets a good brand apart from the rest and keeps you coming back. Your intent is to fulfill your need, and to accomplish that you will want to engage with the brand that will offer you a consistently positive experience, not the one with the lowest price.

There are several principles these brands have in common, and they are consistently executed at all times:

1. A great UX is seamless, with the end user in mind. Make it easy both with product and processes.

2. Time is money. Make sure you are saving your consumer time, both pre-purchase (brand consideration, product features, reviews, purchase process) and post-purchase (returns, credits).

3. Longevity mantra: "It's always easier to take care of current customers than to attract new customers." Too many brands either choose not to engage with their current customers or do not have a process in place to deliver personalized, post-purchase value propositions and value beyond product. Both of these omissions are detriments to long-term, sustainable growth. I am always amazed when I engage with brands, both large and small, that have failed to implement and integrate this into their brand.

4. Take care of your customers, and they will take care of you. Enough said.

5. Simplify your engagement points, empathize and understand your customer. There is nothing worse than a bad purchase experience . . . except for a bad return experience. You may not like the execution of a seamless experience, but it must be the same on both ends of the engagement cycle.

76% of complaints are from having a bad service experience.

Make sure you do not do the same. Be different, be special, be personal.

The touchpoints experienced by a customer are what create your seamless, end-to-end UX cycle. From the outset of this book, I have continually mentioned that visionary brands think beyond an isolated or siloed approach. They analyze the overall UX and how this product will impact their daily lives, but also how to develop it to be user-friendly out of the box. At the very beginning of a product's development, they are asking questions such as:

"How will this make our lives better?"
"Where does it fit?"
"Why are we doing this?"
"What is our POD?"
"When will it be ready?"
"Who will buy this?"

These need to be asked early on, and unless they are cohesively and collectively answered with a clear strategy built around marketplace execution, the answers will not be clear to those you are communicating with. You cannot be at all places at all times, so ensure your voice is translated properly through your consumer engagement, whether online or in person. This can take the form of product marketing literature translated to layman's terms, sites dedicated to brand or product experiences, merchandising, point of purchase, videos, or ambassadors, to name a few. All of this pre-product commercialization planning leads directly to an awesome UX.

Having a visionary UX involves knowing what provides value and inspires your customer so you can create solutions to problems to satisfy this current or future need. A seamless UX is needed for both evolutionary (incremental) and revolutionary (generational) products. Simple sophistication is a method to achieving a great UX through a seamless process. These two words provide a beautiful vision of what engaging with your brands should be for your customers. These consumers can be either proactive (early adopter) or reactive (late adopter). You will need to address both when defining your seamless experience engagement, but each should be the same in the eyes of your brand.

The early adopter is need-driven, while the late adopter is price-driven. There are those in between these groupings, but for the sake of explanation, let's look at both extremes. Being able to satisfy both with a common strategy is the magic formula that makes visionary brands so deadly to compete against. They have mastered this cycle along the adoption curve.

"I want it now." (Early Adopter)

"I can wait." (Late Adopter)

Visionary brands build a system of engagement around the needs of your customer first—those products, technologies, or services they currently need, or what you anticipate they will need in the future. It is the latter that causes the revolution to start and the adoption curve to compress. The compression of the adoption curve has a cause and effect condition on the market, allowing brands to compress the timeline to market. The faster you can commercialize, the faster you can achieve adoption with your new breakaway product. A direct result: rapid revenue growth. A very powerful formula for success, but extremely hard to maintain over a long period of time. Welcome to the world of revolution and continual evolution— evolution that needs to be translated to the world via the UX.

Visionary brands know in order to continue driving the supply and demand curve effectively and efficiently, they must continue to build revolutionary products, balanced with progressive updates. The ongoing success of visionary brands is wrapped around providing for consumer needs and wants. I mention both needs and wants as these two are quite different in how they are translated to the outside world, from a product idea through to eventual consumer adoption.

Being able to bring a vision to reality is a painstaking process few can endure, but if you are able to visualize the end use and how it will make lives better, this will help to drive your passion. Being able to define what is important, while at the same time providing a great UX, should be the goal for any brand, especially those classified as visionary.

ENGAGEMENT

User engagement must happen early and frequently as you provide value to your current or potential customer. Of course, value can take several forms and functions. Most powerfully, it can be offered through personalization, which as we saw in the previous chapter bonds the customer to your brand lifestyle. Everyone wants to feel wanted and understood, no matter what you are selling. The closer you can match an experience to individual need, the closer you come to building a relationship with the customer, eventually turning them into a brand advocate (part of the community) or ambassador (part of the brand).

Engaging with current customers within the loyalty loop, along with securing new consumers, is a delicate balance for brands. Visionary brands use a clearly defined UX and engagement strategy to effectively balance value with acquisition. The value proposition can cross over to the acquisition side, but its connotation is much different as it correlates to lifestyle enhancement versus price point compression. Once a customer has joined the brand community, they will adapt to the brand's product life cycles and choose either *early adopter* or *late adopter* product acquisition timing. A brand's ability to know where their customers are on the adoption curve will tip the marketing investment scales relative to messaging, personalization, and social engagement.

This is a fine art, and being able to read demographic profiles, engage with personalization, and consistently message lifestyle improvements through the adoption cycle will help you attain a loyal base of brand advocates (see previous chapter). These advocates are the ones who allow you to control your brand's destiny . . . but it wasn't always so easy.

Prior to direct-to-consumer channel opportunities, brands would only engage through one-way communications— mailers, flyers, unsolicited e-mails, etc.—none of which allows for the kind of personalization that can be realized today. This is a much different world now, one where brands are in the driver's seat. This is an important shift in our culture, as brands want to control their engagement across all channels (see the Omni-Channel chapter). In controlling their own destiny, they are better able to define all aspects of the purchase loop, marketing, product cycles, engagement platforms, and direct communications.

Of course, this means you need to know how to drive through this shift! Even as your brand is more equipped to secure its own future, there is also the need to understand the intricacies of building, developing, and growing brand awareness and equity. This does not get any easier or less expensive with time, though you now will find there are more tools with which to fine-tune your engine. The digital world we live in waits for no one, so either jump in and start driving or risk getting run over.

Engage with your current customers, stay true to your brand foundation, and build trust and loyalty while advocating the virtues of your products. These current advocates are your company's most valuable asset, and will assist with acquiring new members into your community. They can be measured, they can be engaged, they can be activated . . . or they can be ignored. Ensure you do not ignore—always engage, always provide value beyond product, and you will be rewarded with a mutually beneficial relationship.

Take care of your customers and they will take care of you.

EMPATHIZE

Being able to understand and empathize with your customers brings a personal touch to your creations. Empathy is an understanding of your consumers' world, perceptions, and values, and being able to provide products or solutions which provide for an enhanced lifestyle, either through better products or processes. As discussed within the context of the power triad (product/marketing/sales), you need to ensure everyone understands the purpose behind their products and how your community will eventually utilize this new idea to enhance their everyday life.

This personal touch perspective is reflective of the simple sophistication principle discussed earlier, bringing about your vision of a better way to life—simplicity in the product design, sophistication in how it makes your world better. Visionary brands find this both challenging and enlightening, as it makes you get out of your comfort zone and move into the reality of the solution you are looking to provide. It drives ongoing passion for the product and how it will improve one's life by saving time, improving relationships, or being more efficient or effective. Whatever the motive, creating this product is a labor of love for the brand team.

In defining what creates an attribute worthy of providing empathy for its end user, brands will ask:

Is this a solution looking for a problem, or a problem looking for a solution?

As simple as this question sounds, many brands have fallen short of even asking this question and ventured forward blinded by their own shortsightedness. Finding solutions to everyday problems is an easier path to success, as it can be translated more effectively and realized quicker by end users. The beauty of finding a solution is found in its application in the real world, where the idea becomes reality. In creating solutions, there is a way to connect the community to the brand, and eventually to a product ecosystem fully integrated with their daily life. This drive to join the ecosystem is driven by empathy, as the customer is looking for solutions that are not yet reality but are opportunities to simplify their life. Those brands that embrace this philosophy are ones that understand the needs of their advocates intimately and manifest that understanding through personalization.

Throughout *The Visionary Brand*, we have discussed these vertical brand touchpoints. The more interconnected they become, the more diverse the ecosystem becomes to satisfy the needs of many while personalizing the experience for each. Empathy may seem intangible, but the more tangible a brand makes this connection, the more they find how much their products have impacted individuals, families, and communities across their community.

Empathy is intuition about when something is both right for the brand and can impact a person's life on a genuine level. When you give a person the ability to spend more time at home with the family or with a loved one, this value becomes tangible. Visionary brands understand the impact of this tangible value, and ultimately revenue growth follows. Visionary brands think beyond product; they value the solutions their products provide for their community.

Ultimately, building a visionary-quality UX is about putting together building blocks to form a complex structure of how to engage and interact with your consumer. From the idea through to purchase, you're shooting for a seamless execution of a brand that knows the wants and needs of its customers better than they know it themselves.

Understand your customer. Have empathy for making their life better, find solutions to give them what they currently do not have—more time, family, money, life—and let this empathy fuel your brand's interactions and product pipeline.

This makes you visionary in your customers' eyes and makes your brand a valuable part of their everyday life.

THE NEW AGE

"Distinct or extinct."

– Tom Peters

Generational change has forced brands to evolve . . . or expire. Evolution is the less disruptive cousin of revolutionary change—being able to realize a product that sets the standard for generations is the goal, but few brands bring this vision to reality, and evolution can be just as powerful for a brand's ongoing strategy.

Visionary brands learn to create or adapt products that are superior in design, fit, form, and function in order to satisfy the perpetual expectations of the next generation—the **new age**. The new age has grown up with technological advances that move at light speed, and their expectations are much different than previous generations. Most have never seen an LP record player, a CD, or a cassette player, but they do have an appreciation for the simplicity and culture these creations represent. This appreciation is the artistry visionary brands bring to the new age of products: thought and creation beyond the products themselves, providing valuable function in everyday life. The beauty is in the simplicity of their designs and the absolute power it puts into their hands.

Those visionary brands that embrace these dynamic ideas are the ones that change our world and are positioned best to satisfy the needs of future generations. Looking back, the products that changed the way we interact day-to-day, the ones that made our daily life easier, are the brands that are still around today. They clearly adapted over the years (or failed to do so, in the case of the Walkman, before making an adjustment further down the road), but without having changed their foundational values, positioning, or principles. This can be a tricky balance for companies, and many lie in ruins as a result of not being able to adapt to what comes their way. Anticipation, judgment, and clear decision-making are markers of successful brands that have brought reality to these generational products.

There are two ways to survive these generational shifts through incremental improvements to their core base of products: reimagine the way something is done (**revolution**), or make it substantially better or easier (**evolution**). In many ways the process is very intuitive—the better you know your customer, the easier it is to find solutions to their everyday life issues, sometimes solutions to things they never knew were an issue until the brand provided a proactive solution. This survivor mentality is what drives these great brands to relentlessly execute against a backdrop of change.

Having the ability to see the future needs of your consumers is core to being able to thrive from generation to generation. Great brands, the ones that are still with us today, have this survival mechanism built into their culture, and have a passion for creating and re-creating. While their products are being used in daily lives, their creators have already moved on to the next breakaway idea, which moves them generations ahead. That's the **leadership principle**. Always be thinking, always be different, and others will always look to your brand to lead others within your industry. The competitors will necessarily take up the **follower principle**. Always look to take the lead, and your voice will be the one others follow.

Now the lead dog in a pack, you will run ahead when others are fighting one another for the scraps left behind. Imagine all the freedom realized when you have the lead. Others follow you, most admire you, and future generations will have high expectations for the future you are creating. Staying ahead of this curve is a tricky one to maneuver, though . . . brake too hard (in the form of risk avoidance) and you will allow others to catch up. Come in too hot (risk ignorance) and you will crash and burn. Or simply follow others' lead (commodity) and you will lose your first-mover advantage and your key POD. Ultimately, it is best to strike a balance between revolution and evolution.

If you have a generational lead over your competitors, having mastered product life cycle compression and pushing the demand curve in your favor through ongoing product creation, then inevitably your innovation pipeline will sustain you for a long period of time. But a word of caution: while riding this wave, you must understand the challenges this strategy will pose over the long term. Consistently producing impactful products, reducing commercialization timelines, and providing value to the everyday life of your advocates adds significant pressure to your brand. But integrated correctly, this pressure is what adds to the energy of your brand's continued innovation. With the wind at your back and a clear runway ahead of you, the visionary brand sets a course for others to follow. Generational change, adoption of your creations, and a passion for the brand drive teams to protect their lead at all costs. This is what breeds success inside the minds of your team and flows through your brand's bloodlines.

DISRUPTIVE REVOLUTION

The difference between innovators and imitators is **disruptive revolution**. It is always an easier path to pursue evolutionary products as opposed to revolutionary ones. Both are needed, but only one can be classified as truly innovative.

Those who evolve are those who find ways to provide incremental improvement. Those who create a revolution change your world!

Being disruptive in the new age involves pulling together differing pieces beyond great product and seamless commercialization execution. Disruption in culture, disruption in service, disruption in processes . . . each in its own right can be revolutionary if it substantially improves upon the current status quo. Each is disruptive, but if it is not easily translated to the consumer of the new age, or does not provide a tangible lifestyle enhancement, the adoption rate will suffer.

One aspect needed for disruptive revolution is the ongoing, proactive involvement of your brand advocates combined with a steady stream of new adopters. Losing sight of what is important for each of these groups is a formula for disaster. Visionary brands are constantly, passionately embracing their community, both those who are and those who are not yet brand advocates.

Embracing disruption also means maximizing the sustainable flow of innovative products realized through your creative engine. Each product must be a building block for an ongoing relationship beyond product, and it must be designed to support a lifestyle that brings your customers into the brand, engaging through their products and becoming a loyal part of the community. This community then provides a singular and collective voice embracing what the brand stands for and proactively letting others know of their passion for its creations.

The strategy of disruptive revolution is a part of the new age of generational product adoption through lifestyle enhancement. Brought to life both through products and positioning, this is a powerful strategy when deployed, providing continuous value to the end user through both evolutionary advances in their daily life and revolutionary leaps ahead in how they live their lives.

VISIONARY LEGACY

As covered previously, building a culture of disruption must start at the top, and it must reverberate throughout the brand on a daily basis—it starts with you, the visionary. Whether verbal or visual, every message you send must both build passion for the brand and firmly entrench your foundational principles. It is this infectious attitude that contains the formula for a successful long-term relationship with the brand. It flows through product use and lifestyle status to become a part of their culture, their community.

Generational change requires visionary leaders who are inspirational, authentic, and compassionate. Being able to master these qualities is what separates visionaries from mere executives. These leaders leave a legacy for others to embrace, and for future brand leaders to follow.

I have seen through direct observation of visionary brands that the impact of such a leader ripples through the entire brand. Passionate inspiration blends with far-reaching vision.

In blazing their own trail, they provide a path for the future of the brand.

Always be cutting your own path, but always ensure you are leaving a clear legacy for others. This provides for the ability to look back and see how what you are today was built from what is behind. This will take you down many paths and many obstacles, most of which will make you a better brand, company, or person.

Swim where others dare not go, keep true to your past, but leave a legacy for the future. Find your open water, your blue ocean. That is where your legacy lies. There are plenty of opportunities for achieving your legacy; all you need to do is have the courage to pursue your revolutionary idea. This is your chance to leave a legacy, to change the world for the better.

THE ARTIST

"I set as a goal the maximum capacity that people have—I settle for no less. I make myself a relentless architect of the possibilities of human beings."

– Benjamin Zander, Conductor, Boston Philharmonic

When Steve Jobs was brought back to revitalize the company he had co-founded, he made a lot of unexpected changes. But what was most surprising was who he hired to help bring Apple back from the brink of extinction: along with all the engineers and builders and other technical experts, he hired **artists**.

In retrospect, this was a genius move. Apple could bring in the smartest technical geniuses in the industry to make the most advanced software . . . but if it didn't make sense on an aesthetic, human level, then who would want to buy it? That was one of the most revolutionary facets of Steve Jobs' visionary approach: brands are made up of people and succeed or fail based on the actions of people. The ability to see beyond the product and embrace this human touch is a creator mentality. No brand can aspire to visionary status without a thorough consideration of the human factor at all levels.

Artistry is something that can often go overlooked even now, even with Apple's example to look back on. The fact of the matter is that the human perspective is a subtle thing, and not something easily understood by everyone. Marketing, packaging, UX—in every aspect of how your community interacts with your brand, the difference between success and failure can be as minor as a font choice, a specific shade of a color, the phrasing of an email or advertisement.

To cut to the chase: if your brand is staffed with the best and brightest technical minds to the exclusion of artists and other creative, human-focused experts, it's going to lose the human element, the simple sophistication of daily interaction with a machine or service.

Ultimately, though, artistry is about more than just hiring artists—as the leader of a visionary brand, you need to cultivate a certain amount of artistry in yourself and every member of your team, to one degree or another. Bringing artistry into a brand requires being able to find the artistry in others, and understanding how they all blend together to create beautiful music. At the crossroads of culture, diversity, and creation is a beautiful orchestration conducted by visionaries who see the value in collective artistry. You need a seamless execution created by a team that complements each other's skillsets to put everyone in a position to succeed as a team. The poets, the rebels, the creators, the observers—each needs a place in your brand, and each needs the freedom and support to let the creative juices flow. What you need is a machine made up of passionate individuals organized to turn their talents towards bringing about an improved life, an enhanced experience, or the simple sophistication of something difficult made easier.

If you're going to nurture the artist in yourself, you're going to need to look beyond the world of your brand. After all, at the end of the day, you're not just a leader, you're a human being, and bringing more of a human touch to your brand is only going to work if you get in touch with your own artistry . . . and thus, your own humanity.

So just how are you supposed to make an artist out of yourself? The trick is to lean into the strengths and passions you already have—the artist in each of us is unique, and understanding our distinctive God-given skills is key to finding our passion. Start building that creator mentality in your everyday life. Observe your daily interactions with tools, technology, or products people use every day. Ask why we do it this way and how it can be made better. This is the creative process: creating meaningful products for the betterment of society or individuals. And it's built on an understanding of the human emotion or touch, the impact on someone's day-to-day life. That's the artistry behind the product.

Artistry can be best illustrated through an actual artist who translated his work to art, his passion to reality. Vincent van Gogh was planning to be a clergyman with no thoughts of becoming an artist, a skill he had not yet discovered. We are fortunate that he discovered his passion, and how he translates the *why* is enlightening as well.

In looking at what inspired van Gogh, it was not the careful, well-thought-out process of design, the balance of color or shapes, or worrying about whether it would sell; it was his creative instinct that drove him. He had a passion for creating something beautiful he could share with others. His artistry was always driven by this passion, and that passion is why today his art commands the value it does. Van Gogh did not create these masterpieces for the money—he earned $109 with his art during his lifetime—but rather that we might stop long enough to see the artistry that is around us. His every creation was driven by being authentic, genuinely embracing what he was painting and sharing this with others. Build that own authentic passion for what you do and for your life principles (see "The Courage") and it will shine through in your work.

> "Great things are done by a series of small things brought together."
>
> – *Vincent van Gogh*

We rarely share our thoughts in our own work, much less discuss the thoughts in the artistry that is around us. It would do us all good to share our thoughts and our passions with others in order that they too will be inspired with their own passion. Van Gogh was able to create genuine art, pieces no one can replicate as no one can recreate his passion for his work. Van Gogh did not worry about the skeptics, but rather wanted to share the beauty he saw with the world.

Be an artist, live life with a passion and share it with others.

"What would life be if we had no courage to attempt anything?"

– Vincent van Gogh

Understanding the impact of your creation on society and culture will allow you to better understand the ongoing value provided to those who use your products. Think of revolutionary, generational products that affected your daily life and how you embrace them, either professionally or personally. The area most overlooked by companies is in the value their products provide beyond functional use—look to how products like the iPhone influence your lifestyle and how you interact with co-workers, family and friends. Not all products will have this type of impact, but visionary ones do, and anything is possible when you connect the dots between functional use and lifestyle enhancement.

In creating great products that change our daily lives, and how we interact with others is difficult, the music is hard to write and more difficult to play, but true artists find it enlightening and are able to translate this passion for life to reality in the real world. The artist is a key piece of the brand orchestration and plays a pivotable role in ensuring the reality of real-world experiences is brought to life.

> "I am always doing that which I cannot do, in order that I may learn how to do it."
>
> – *Pablo Picasso*

Play your music—be a creator and be yourself. Being genuinely engaged while living life passionately should be your ultimate goal.

Visionary brands put the right people on the right instrument, whether through their inherent skill set, passion, or both. Too often those who think they can play (marketing, sales, product, etc.) are a detriment to the entire team when they reach beyond the role they need to fill in the overall ensemble. Be a creator, be part of a team, and know the role you play for the overall success of the brand.

If needed, the visionary leader will rearrange the orchestra so each can play together as one . . . a true *masterpiece.* Being able to put the right people on the right instrument and have them play beautifully in unison with one another leads to a rich, rewarding experience for the instrumentalist (team), the conductor (company) and the audience (customer). This will lead to a harmonious, thriving brand culture.

Know your role, have a passion for what you do, and support others throughout the process. This leads to the enviable result of having those who are part of the brand feel they *are* the brand. This feeling is the lifeblood of the creators—the true, passionate artists.

THE COURAGE

"We must build dikes of courage to hold back the
flood of fear."

– Martin Luther King, Jr.

There are business principles and there are **life principles**. These are mutually exclusive, but they work in parallel to define who we are as a person or brand. Finding a way to stay true to both will lead to a more prosperous, kind, and giving life, both personally and professionally. Not merely making the effort, but genuinely, willfully caring about what you are doing makes all the difference. We've covered a lot of the business principles already, so let's look at how life principles can and should influence how your brand operates in a visionary way.

Truly visionary brands live by their principles every day. Their principles provide insight into the daily lives of their teams, communities, and those they touch in life. Finding a purpose beyond work is a proactive principle of visionary brands—to find a need and fill it, to give back. You must find a purpose for your team beyond product, beyond the brand, beyond their role in order to energize them to protect the ethos of what you stand for as a company.

In fact, living life through the lens of a brand that has an aspirational vision is both rewarding and satisfying. Visionary brands know in order to attract talent, you must have a **purpose beyond product**.

Having a purpose beyond product involves creating a culture within a brand, driven by a collective goal to make a difference in the lives of those you touch. How you touch your community and beyond is driven by the foundational character of the brand you support or work for. Working together for a common goal creates an environment driven by interdependence and collective execution, not independence or selfishness. Visionary brands have embraced this interdependence culture as the livelihood of their purpose continues to grow. It is then nurtured by those associated with the brand, those who understand its ethos. Having this type of commitment to collective interdependence breeds an environment of trust, engagement, and reliance on each other.

As Stephen Covey put it in his book *The 7 Habits of Highly Effective People*:

"Human life is **interdependent**! We can combine our talents and abilities and create something greater together. Interdependent people combine their own efforts with the efforts of others to achieve their greatest success."

Being able to create, build, and set this foundation and ensuring it is protected is a common lifeline with visionary brands. This is what breathes life into an otherwise stale company, and this sort of selfless, purpose-driven foundation can be realized through the following life principles:

- **Faith** – Belief in the right things will become reality.
- **Hope** – The future will be bright and good will prevail.
- **Charity** – Actively help and care for others.
- **Diligence** – *Never* give up.
- **Kindness** – Be fair and equitable with others.
- **Prudence** – Show care and moderation with money.
- **Temperance** – Practice moderation in things that are needed, remove things that are not.

These principles are what make up the heart and soul of a visionary brand. We have discussed many areas that are characteristics of a visionary brand, but it is the **character** of a great brand that sustains them during the ups and downs. Having these at the heart of your brand, ingrained into your leaders, will serve as a unified purpose for the brand as a whole.

In observing various brands, I have found dedication to these core life principles to be a common weak point, one that prevents them from achieving visionary status. By not being authentic, by doing something only because it is what you are expected to do, brands create an atmosphere of cynicism that seeps into the culture of the brand. When living up to these life principles, you must make a personal commitment to upholding these principles throughout your brand. Leaders understand a simple fact:

Take care of those who support you, and they will take care of you.

This is a life principle that affects both life and career. In promoting and embracing this manifestation of servant leadership, the brand itself benefits. However, you can't force it for those who do not wish to support others; in the long run, they will suffer for it, and this selfish trait usually carries on throughout their career. Your team will benefit from having authentically, passionately embraced this leadership quality and style, but you can't force it.

In order to move ahead you must take care of those behind you and work with those in front of you. Nobody survives on an island by themselves; we need other people to make it work. Visionary leaders embrace those who join their company and community. They are constantly finding genuine ways through rewards, events, promotions, and products to keep them engaged. Remember, a complacent brand is a dying brand. Always move ahead, always look for ways to drive the passion of your foundational principles into your culture every day. It is not enough to say you are committed; you must show your passion through actual action, both visual and verbal.

> "Whether you think you can,
> or you think you can't—you're right."
>
> *– Henry Ford*

Visionary brands understand the role life principles play in defining who they are and what they can achieve. **Faith** is what lets us believe that things will work toward success and even a setback will move you forward, setting the stage for a clear path for others to follow.

> "Faith is taking the first step, even when you do not see the entire staircase."
>
> *– Martin Luther King, Jr.*

On top of all the other life principles, make sure you have the **courage** to carry you down the path to success. The courage to be different is where most companies are not comfortable venturing. However, in order to be different, you must *be different*. Visionary brands have this built into their foundation, and this is what makes them unique. The courage to be different is also what provides for a diverse cultural experience and richly rewarding career for those lucky enough to be entrenched in their world. These brands are winners; they have calculated, conveyed, and implemented a brand ethos across all levels of the company, which bleeds into their communities. Loyalty, trust, experience, and lifestyle—all are important to everyone, regardless of race or religion.

Having a positive attitude, providing the right tools, and evangelizing your cultural foundation will allow for the courage and faith you will need to carry on through the rough waters ahead. There is always a light at the end of the road; make progress, have faith, and always hold true to your foundation, as it will sustain you during these times. Remember, a failure always moves you closer to success . . .

"Success is not final, failure is not fatal; it is the courage to continue that counts."

– *Sir Winston Churchill*

These life principles anchor a visionary brand. They are inherently personal, but they can and should be reflected in your brand's bloodlines. Everyone associated with your brand needs to have the courage to venture where others have not gone, the faith to believe that with perseverance you will see your vision brought to reality, and the **hope** that the lives of those in your community will ultimately be bettered by your creation.

Other values important to longevity are rooted in being part of and proactively embracing social awareness through charity, kindness, and servant leadership. Each is important independent of the others, but collectively they provide value beyond the company itself. Rich experiences and consistent foundational values will provide value beyond those things which are tangible.

These values go beyond the walls of visionary brands, and are consistently embraced within these companies' corridors.

These life principles are part of a visionary brand's core values. They drive the day-to-day for everyone who is part of their company, both inside and out. Living life beyond product is what visionary brands bring to their teams, community, and advocates. They are selling a lifestyle, yes, but they also have a choice in deciding what is important to the brand. To live up to their status, they must choose to consistently anchor the brand in these principles in all it does on a global scale.

DESTINY

Like a ship setting sail, there can only be one captain, but they need the support of all around them. After all, the crew all has the same goal: move along the charted path, steer the ship away from danger, correct the path, and collectively proceed towards the destination.

This is true for visionary brands as well: with the guidance of the captain (their visionary leader) and their plan (their foundational principles), they stay the course, learning how to avoid danger without shying away from it.

Knowing you must take risk in order to achieve success is your first step towards becoming visionary. Your initial step will be learning how to sail your ship into danger, not knowing what is next other than your eventual destination, and you must take quick, decisive action when you are taken off course by the next storm. There will be many storms, and the ability to adapt, learn, and integrate to ensure you are better prepared for the next storm will be a key factor in determining your destiny.

Many companies do not learn from the past and choose stubbornly to continue to stay the course without adapting. Eventually there will come a time when the next storm is too much and they have not prepared properly, leading to their demise.

Take risks, learn from your mistakes, adapt, and integrate.

Continue to be diligent, never giving up on your vision. This is the path of most resistance, but the difficulty is made easier by your commitment. If your foundation is strong, your vision tangible, and your cause worthy, then your path will be made easier by having a team to support your success. A captain is only as good as their team, and an idea is only as good as the paper it is written on. Have the diligence to set your course and the desire to see what lies ahead, but also maintain the intelligence to know the danger that awaits as you move towards your destiny.

Visionary brands—the ones that have sustained a long history of success—know who they are, where they are going, and how they will get there. What's more, they are always committed to reaching their destination. They have a strong leader: a visionary committed to maintaining and evangelizing the brand's foundational values, building an inclusive culture where all work in concert with one another to reach their destination. Together they achieve what they never thought was possible until they came together to achieve a dream. Those who come together in this journey represent the true spirit of a visionary brand.

LIVE YOUR DREAM

Life is too short to not have a plan. Visionary brands and the visionaries themselves recognize this need. That's what your vision is, really—a dream that you, and only you, can turn into a plan.

I have found visionary brands recognize the challenges they face, providing clear direction and ensuring everyone clearly understands the path ahead. The road is not easily traversed; many times you are the trailblazer, surveying difficult terrain, and many times you will have to change course . . . but never direction. You have a clear direction, and in order to execute your vision you must always be making progress. Being able to recognize when you are making progress versus lingering in a state of denial is what separates failure from success. There is a direct correlation between frustration and following the status quo, and this is why having a culture of risk and eventual failure is an integral piece of a visionary brand's foundational core. As with a rip current, you will not always know when you are in danger until it is too late. Do not get blindsided, understand what is ahead, be proactive in setting your path, and keep making progress.

I hope this book has inspired you on your journey, and as you move along in your career and your life, never forget the two are intertwined. Make sure to take time to relax, listen to the music, live life, and enjoy the ride!

Your destiny awaits . . . !

SUMMARY

All great visionary brands started with a great idea and did not give up until this idea became reality. Each had a mindset of never giving up, never letting the idea pass if it furthered their cause, and they each established themselves as the disruptor, the leader, the one who inspires.

Along the journey to my eventual destination, I compiled more than my fair share of stories—happy stories, sad stories, inspiring stories. Taken as a whole, they paint a picture of what a visionary brand can truly be. I am sure as you voyage along your own path you will also have your own adventures, challenges, and inspirations—each a valuable learning experience.

Embrace failure, learn from failure, and realize your dreams . . .

Where there is no risk, there is no reward . . .

There were many people who inspired me along the way, from my parents to my family and the leaders from all these truly visionary brands. Without these leaders who blazed their own path, there would be no path to eventual success. These visionaries have inspired the great young brands today, and the legacy of their creations is carried on through the foundational principles that allowed them to survive and thrive in good times and bad.

The ability to sustain and maintain their vision— The Visionaries . . .

There will be many to follow, many who will hopefully gain knowledge from the adventures of others who have completed this journey. Over difficult mountain peaks and through valleys of despair, they will need to stick to their values, maintain integrity, and stay true to who they are as a brand. This is what creates both loyalty and longevity, and both are required to sustain success. These qualities—this vision—is what sustains brands, what allows them to grow beyond their sight and what anchors them in a foundation that does not crumble.

"The noblest pleasure is the joy of understanding."

– Leonardo da Vinci

This **Journey** to visionary status starts with defining the foundational pillars of the brand, understanding your role as a brand leader, and executing on the elements that make up a successful **Formula**.

As we discussed in **The Creative Engine,** your ideas must be converted to market-driving products that disrupt an industry. These revolutionary products are then **Positioned** at premium level and marketed vertically through your **Omni-Channel Strategy**. Once commercialized, the brand vision is realized through the collaborative efforts of your **Power Triad** (product/marketing/sales). Don't stop loading the **Fuel** into the brand engine as you continue disrupting categories, building markets, and eliminating competition with this new pipeline of innovative, breakaway products. These ideas are carried through to the **New Age** with an enhanced, value-driven **User Experience**. All of these elements make up the formula for long-term success. Although difficult, you have a roadmap, a path that has been carved by others for you to follow. Have passion for what you do, and support others through courageous servant leadership.

Visionary brands are constantly reloading, fine-tuning, and evangelizing those inside and outside the brand, providing those who play their instruments the proper tools for them to succeed in their roles. This leads to the enviable result of having those who are part of the brand feel they ARE the brand. This is the lifeblood of creators.

The **Foundational Principles** that make up a visionary brand are both inspirational and aspirational. In order to have a brand that your employees, your community, and your peers admire, you must come through the fire of competition, the challenge of consistent creation, and the demands of maintaining your commitment to your values and your **Life Principles** through all circumstances.

The intent of *The Visionary Brand* is to help you recognize all the differing areas within your company that need to be nurtured—each is a part of this living, breathing thing we call a brand. These foundational principles need to be cared for in order for your brand to achieve the level of success achieved by others that have set the standard. Each of these building blocks to achieving your visionary brand is essential and must be constantly pursued from the top down.

Whether you're just starting out, have an insanely great idea, or have an established brand, I hope you have found this book to be enlightening, inspirational, and aspirational in building your future success. Good luck, and never forget to remain true to who you are as you disrupt the market with products that will influence how we live for generations!

INDEX

adidas, 11, 40, 56, 78, 82, 142, 164

Albert Einstein, 46, 148

Andrew Carnegie 8, 46

Apple, 14, 29, 52, 58–9, 65, 73, 95, 122–3, 136, 140, 142, 158, 192–3

artist, 37, 51, 120, 157–8, 186, 192–8

aspiration, 16–7, 78–80, 82, 145, 153, 162–6, 200, 213

authenticity, 21–2, 44–5, 62, 74, 79, 105, 121, 123–4, 128, 169–70, 195

Bill Gates, 8

Billabong, 2

bloodlines, 5, 61–3, 76, 104–5, 139, 163

brand advocates, 20, 43, 60, 82, 108, 144, 179, 189

breakaway, 29–31, 47, 74, 96, 114, 124–31, 134–6, 140, 142, 159

cannibalization, 53, 142

character, 44, 106, 112–3, 200, 202

commodity, 16, 18, 55, 66, 68, 73, 75, 79–80, 155

courage, 9, 33, 37, 47, 140, 199, 204–5

crazy ones, 35, 46, 88

creator, 24, 147, 158, 193–4, 197–8

culture, 2, 104, 107–11, 198

Culture Matrix, 80, 104–7, 112–6

destiny, 17, 159, 162, 206–7

diligence, 23, 201, 207

disruption, 3–4, 42, 45–8, 52–4, 88, 92–3, 102–3, 121, 125–6, 147, 149, 152–4, 163, 189–90

diversity, 113, 183, 194, 204

drawdown, 30, 76–7, 126, 131–9, 141–2

dream, 47, 126, 208–9

ecosystem, 52–3, 95, 156–60, 183

Elon Musk, 49

engagement, 20–2, 31, 56, 64–9, 71–2, 82–3, 161–2, 166, 176–7, 179–81

ensemble, 6, 197

ethos, 44, 58, 60, 119, 141, 152, 204

evolution, 19–21, 33–4, 43, 90, 153, 178, 185–8

extinction, 139–43, 185

eyewear, 1–2

failure, 13, 18, 25, 28, 35, 53–4, 80, 87, 98, 100, 103, 121, 126, 148–50153, 204

fear, 9, 21, 53, 59–60, 86, 199

first-mover advantage, 31, 42–3, 80, 92, 103, 123, 159, 188

follower, 59, 121, 140, 187

foresight, 14, 29, 32–4, 42, 50, 53, 118, 157

foundational pillars, 3–5, 7, 24–6, 36, 47–8, 212

fuel, 90, 149, 161–6, 169, 173, 212

generational product, 14, 118–9, 186, 190, 196

Henry Ford, 28, 46, 154, 203

imitate, 33, 77, 119–20, 123–4, 133, 138, 189

Innovators Curve, 53–4

inspiration, 52, 120, 140, 144, 162, 164–5, 166–7, 191, 213

interdependent, 93, 201

Jeff Bezos, 8

Jim Jannard, 59, 162–3

John D. Rockefeller, 8, 46

legacy, 190–1, 211

lifestyle, 7, 11, 16–8, 21, 40, 62, 64, 67, 70, 73, 78–80, 82–3, 88–9, 91, 107, 110, 139, 147, 153, 164–5, 173, 180, 190, 197, 205

loyalty loop, 21–2, 65, 66–72, 85, 106, 179

market-driving products, 30, 42–5, 96, 128, 150

marketing, 19, 43, 69, 94–5, 99–101, 131, 135, 161–2, 165–6, 180

Martin Luther King Jr., 199, 203

Moveable Weight Technology, 74–5, 132

NCAA, 11

New Age, 17, 67, 69, 185–7, 190, 212

Nicola Tesla, 46

Oakley, 1–4, 11, 59, 78, 102–3, 114–5, 162–3

omni-channel, 19–20, 55, 71, 82–91, 212

personalization, 53, 56–7, 66–71, 85, 106, 166–9, 179–80, 183

Pablo Picasso, 120, 197

POD (Point of Difference), 64–6, 99, 107, 111, 138, 188

positioning, 19, 24, 55–66, 73, 78–81, 90–1, 94, 95–6, 105, 107–8, 115, 122, 130, 144, 146–7, 153,

Power Triad, 92–103, 108, 125, 134, 161, 182

premium status, 18, 55, 62–6, 68, 70, 73–7, 80, 107–8, 117, 131–3, 161, 166

principles, 6, 19, 25–6, 71, 101, 104–5, 108–9, 116, 144, 151–2, 161, 175–6, 190, 199–205, 213

product lifecycle, 117, 134, 139–42, 148

product pipeline, 29–31, 121, 124, 131–4, 139–44, 188

product squeeze, 73–5, 77–8, 95

Quiksilver, 2, 60–1

Ralph Lauren, 78, 107, 164

recreate, 33–5, 147, 196

retention, 22, 56

revolutionary mindset, 34–5, 129, 178, 185–7, 196

risk, 12–3, 32–5, 46, 48, 53, 98, 118, 121, 139, 147, 148–55, 187–8, 206–7, 211

servant leadership, 110–2, 202, 205, 212

Sony, 29, 52, 140

soul, 57–61, 124, 202

Steve Jobs, 7–8, 14, 29, 35, 46, 122, 136, 142, 144, 153, 192–3

synergy, 39, 96, 161

TaylorMade, 11, 74–5, 131–3, 142

Thomas Edison, 46, 96, 117

trust, 7, 22–4, 40, 44–5, 57–8, 60, 89, 100, 106, 112–3, 124, 164, 181, 201

Under Armour, 4, 99

UX (User Experience), 17, 31, 66, 126, 146, 157, 168, 174–81

Vincent van Gogh, 195–7

Walkman, 29, 52–3, 140, 144, 186

Winston Churchill, 204

ABOUT THE AUTHOR

Bryan Smeltzer is a seasoned executive and authentic entrepreneur. He started his career in the aerospace industry working in the stealth program, then quickly moved into consumer products, starting his own apparel company and eventually selling to a VC firm.

He has held executive roles in some of the world's most iconic brands such as Oakley, K-Swiss, TaylorMade, and adidas, going on to lead global business development, product, and marketing for these and other brands. Currently Bryan is leading LiquidMind, Inc., a global brand strategy firm located in southern California.

BryanSmeltzer.com

LiquidMindsite.com

The Visionary Chronicles PODCAST

www.ingramcontent.com/pod-product-compliance
Lightning Source LLC
Chambersburg PA
CBHW070657190326
41458CB00053B/6916/J